A GENTLE TOUCH

A GENTLE TOUCH

*From a theology of handicap to a
theology of human being*

David A. Pailin

First published in Great Britain 1992
SPCK
Holy Trinity Church
Marylebone Road
London NW1 4DU

British Library Cataloguing in Publication Data

A catalogue record for this book is available
from the British Library

ISBN 0-281-04575-5

Typeset by Pioneer Associates Ltd, Perthshire
Printed in Great Britain by
Biddles Ltd, Guildford and Kings Lynn

ALEXANDER MARK BERRY
4 May 1987 – 20 June 1988

EI
GRATIAS
DEO

Contents

Preface

Handicap itself is not necessarily a form of suffering. Some forms of handicap, such as blindness, cystic fibrosis and infertility, are clearly a source of distress to those who find themselves so afflicted. Not all handicapped people, however, are to be regarded as suffering simply because they are handicapped. Every case of handicap as such probably only appears to be a form of the problem of evil to those who consider their own supposedly non-handicapped state as the norm of what it is to be human, or who consider that people cannot be happy who do not share their skills and interests.

Such a judgement reminds me of the way in which one of my friends considers that my life is blighted because I do not enjoy the taste of brandy while I wonder why she is not fascinated with the intellectual puzzles posed by rational reflection on belief in God! These differences are part of the rich variety of human being. They do not show her or me to be less than fully human. It is even more unjustified to consider that handicapped people lack what is needed for fully human existence. To regard them in this way implies that they are in a state which ideally needs 'repair' or 'correction' or 'amendment' in order for them to be fully human. This is a mistaken as well as a patronizing judgement. It fails to recognize, firstly, that all of us are limited; secondly, that handicapped people are persons in their own right; thirdly, that there is no ideal mode of human existence, let alone a fixed one that remains constant whatever the cultural context; and fourthly – and above all – that from the divine perspective non-handicapped people are likely to be no more creatively significant than handicapped people.

A Fellow of the Royal Society may smile at how in understanding physics a second former feels superior to a first former. Both have much to discover! Similarly the way in which the non-handicapped (in their own estimation) may often consider themselves superior to the handicapped may seem to God amusing, ignorant and trivial. God enjoys as richly the achievement of a baby in managing to sit up as the excitement of a scientist in achieving a breakthrough in understanding.

The first chapter explains why this book has been written. There is no need to anticipate that story here. I hope, however, that the way in which my brief encounter with Alex challenged my ideas and provoked this book may stimulate others to reflect fruitfully on what faith should affirm about what it is to be a human being and how each human being is related to God. There are, however, four people to whom thanks are due. Firstly, I am very grateful to Jackie and Michael Berry, the parents of Alex, for their interest and support in the development of this study. I am very sensible of their grace in allowing me to focus my thought on Alex. They are, however, in no way to be held responsible for the theological conclusions that I have reached. Secondly, Arnold Anderson, a former colleague at the University of Manchester, a great friend and a percipient scholar, has wrestled with me on these issues, reading each draft carefully, challenging my ideas and suggesting further lines of reflection. I thank him for his ungrudging help and intellectual stimulation, his humour, and his persistent threats to a sensible diet! He is not to be blamed for my failure to take full advantage of his advice. Thirdly, Judith Longman deserves thanks for her patience with an author who dismally failed to meet the successive deadlines which he offered! Finally, my thanks go to Alex for all that his gentle touch has brought me to see. I would like to say that this is his book but I do not want him, any more than anyone else, to be burdened with responsibility for my ideas. Therefore I dedicate it to him.

David A. Pailin
11 August 1991

1

How it all started

Alexander changed my understanding. It was not through anything he said – he never spoke any words – nor through anything in particular that he did. I do not know much about him. I only met him – and then briefly – on a few occasions. Nevertheless, simply by being who he was he made me think again about what it is to be human and about how human beings find their ultimate worth in their relationship to God. Alex's touch was gentle; it was also profound.

If, as has recently been suggested, revelation can be described as 'a conversion of the imagination' (Green 1989: 68), Alex has been for me a source of revelation. This is not to claim divine inspiration, let alone divine authorship, for the thoughts which have emerged. It is to confess that my encounter with Alex has been, to use another theologian's phrase, a 'disclosure situation' (cf. Ramsey 1964; 1965). For this I am grateful to him.

This book has been written that others may consider the ideas which Alex has provoked in me. It is not a comprehensive treatise on the issues which it raises. Conversations have shown me that what is here discussed raises many further questions. What I have written will have succeeded in part if it lures others into thinking and writing about them. Nor is this book intended to be a technical theological study with numerous references and critical responses to the works of others. Its aim is to make some basic affirmations about being human from a perspective informed by reflecting on the condition of certain persons who are members of the human community.

What is said in the following chapters may seem so obvious that anyone with common sense and a realistic faith in God should be aware of its truth. Why, then, make these points? Firstly, they are worth stating because faith's convictions and theological understanding sometimes fail to meet the proper demands of common sense and rational credibility.

Alex made me realize that things I had affirmed did not stand up to critical reflection. Secondly, what is so obvious that it does not seem worth stating may be so obvious that it is overlooked. Those travelling to Jerusalem should take care not to be so taken up with the fine points of priestly devotion and Levitical practice that they do not notice a person in distress. In the quest for understanding we must not be so allured by the mysterious that we miss the truth confronting us. Thirdly, it may be that some of the points which I make here are not generally obvious and uncontroversial. Hardly anything is in faith and theology! Readers will have to make up their own minds on this – by reading this book!

These, however, are teasing comments. What lies behind them?

During the Easter vacation in 1987 I made the final revisions to my contribution to a volume of essays to be published the following summer (Pailin 1988). The collection was an attempt by a small group of Methodist theologians to respond to the celebrations of the two hundred and fiftieth anniversary of John Wesley's experience at a meeting house in Aldersgate Street. Interpretations of this event as one of 'conversion', although widespread, may owe more to nineteenth-century American revivalist mythology about the events of 24 May 1738 than to scholarly research. In any case, whatever the significance of Wesley's experience of a 'strangely warmed heart', the members of the group hoped to show that some Methodists had clear heads!

My contribution is entitled 'The Poet of Salvation'. In it I maintain that various traditional views of salvation are now neither significant nor credible. They present the human need of salvation in ways with which many people today are unable to identify. Such people do not see themselves as slaves to cosmic powers, nor as having offended the divine honour, nor as debtors who cannot pay the penalties for having broken divine rules. And just as such diagnoses of fundamental human need fail to be significant, so the corresponding descriptions of its remedy are incredible. To use notions of payment of ransom to a kidnapper, defeat of a usurper, satisfaction of feudal honour, and conformity to administrative regulations to interpret God's saving activity is to envisage it in ways that are not compatible with the divine holiness, ultimacy and perfection. Even as models or metaphors such views of the fundamental need of human existence and of the divine response to it are inadequate.

How, then, should that need be perceived? In my essay I suggest that it should be perceived as the need to establish the significance of human being – and this means the life of each person – in face of the physical, historical and individual challenges posed by its situation. Physically, human being appears to be only a brief excursus in the development of the cosmos; historically, human achievements decay into oblivion; individually, we are products of the accidents of inheritance and are finite in our potentialities. The cry for salvation is the cry for worth and meaning in the face of these threats.

Having thus identified what may credibly be understood as the need of salvation, I then turn in the essay to consider what may similarly be understood as God's response to the human predicament. How is the character of divine salvation to be perceived? In outlining what may appear to some believers to be a revisionary conception of 'salvation' (although it is a view which can claim to have a good pedigree), I take up Whitehead's description of God as 'saving' the world by preserving the values that are achieved in it and, as 'the poet of world, with tender patience leading it by his vision of truth, beauty and goodness' (Whitehead 1978: 346).

Two things are affirmed here about the character of divine salvation. One is that God's saving activity is to be understood as God's unlimited awareness and preservation (in the divine memory) of each momentary event. As the panentheistic understanding of God perceives (cf. Pailin 1989: 76ff.), whatever anyone experiences, whatever anyone feels, whatever anyone does, it is embraced by God. Therefore it never perishes. It contributes its qualities to God's everlasting reality. We thus have the satisfaction of knowing that our present joys are for ever joys in God. The other aspect of salvation is that God responds to each present situation by seeking to draw out of it future creative achievements and aesthetic satisfactions. This is done by presenting human beings with visions of truth, beauty and goodness. These visions make them discontent with their

present state; they stir them to creative activity. I thus
conclude that 'God "saves" by preserving what people have
achieved and by evoking in them creative responses to their
situation' (Pailin 1988: 46).

Then Alex was born. As I thought about him I became
aware that what I had written about salvation was basically
flawed. And it was not just that my understanding of
salvation was flawed. The need for rethinking went deeper. I
had to think again about what it is to be human and, in
particular, what the self-understanding of faith declares
about the significance of human life as established by the
relationship between human beings and God.

In many ways the particular details of Alex's life are not
important for this study, and most of them I do not know. I
have no reason to know them. Since, however, it may help
readers to grasp the nature of the issues discussed in this
book if they know something of the concrete reality of the
events which provoked my thinking, here is a short
description of Alex's life which his mother wrote and which
his parents have allowed me to include.

About Alex

Alexander was born in St Mary's Hospital, Manchester, four
weeks premature, on 4 May 1987, by caesarian section as it
was thought he might not survive a normal delivery. He was
smaller than expected for his gestational age and had Down's
Syndrome. He spent the first twenty-four hours in oxygen in
an incubator but subsequently made good progress and after
eight days on the Special Care Baby Unit (SCBU) was
transferred to the ward. He was eventually allowed home ten
days later – he still weighed less than five pounds. Five days
later he was readmitted to hospital with severe jaundice.
After exhaustive tests, which found no obvious cause, he
required a blood transfusion. For four weeks he had twice-
weekly blood tests but the jaundice remained. He was booked
to go to theatre on 1 July for a liver biopsy for suspected
biliary atresia; remarkably, he started to improve the
weekend before the proposed operation, on the Sunday of
which he was baptized.

The weeks of jaundice, however, seemed to have caused

problems with Alex's bone formation and on 2 August he was readmitted to St Mary's and found to have spontaneous fractures of two ribs and his right arm. He was discharged after further investigations but twelve days later was readmitted with a severe chest infection, a distended bowel and suspected whooping cough. For the next eleven days he was fed through a tube and kept in an oxygen tent, with no improvement, and he broke another rib. On Sunday 30 August he suffered a respiratory and cardiac arrest and was transferred to the SCBU and put on ventilation. He was not expected to live. After two further arrests he was suffering fits, for which he required medication, and he had two more broken ribs. Three days later he spat out the ventilation tube, during routine maintenance, and he never looked back! He was discharged from hospital on 9 September, having had a second blood transfusion but requiring no other medication. The only obvious sign of trauma was his loss of voice – you could only tell if he was crying by looking at him.

During October and November Alex had further stays in St Mary's Hospital, both times with chest infections. At this time he was also found to have a hole in his heart which required medication. Two weeks before Christmas he was again admitted to hospital, this time for surgery on an inguinal hernia and for a rectal biopsy, as he was still troubled by bowel distention and constipation. He again spent some time on the SCBU, but made a rapid recovery.

From Christmas until March Alex made good progress. He put on some weight, and enjoyed standing, shaking hands, and bouncing with support, and became a champion bubble-blower!

At the beginning of March Alex was admitted to St Mary's for cardiac catheterization. He was found to have a one centimetre hole between the atria and to have very severe pulmonary hypertension. Despite this, a week later he had a second bowel biopsy operation. He was never really well again.

In April he was admitted to St Mary's from The Royal Manchester Children's Hospital, Pendlebury, having turned blue. He was found to have another chest infection and to have developed another hernia. Also, he was finally diagnosed as having Hirschprung's Disease, a condition where there are no nerves to the lower part of the bowel, causing constipation, distention and extreme discomfort. After his first birthday Alex was dashed to hospital several times, having gone blue, and finally was admitted to the intensive care unit of The Royal Manchester Children's Hospital, where he died on Monday 20 June at 7.30 p.m.

We give thanks to God for the life of Alex, who despite everything was happy and cheerful and seemed to have a special magic.

We thank God also for the doctors, nurses and others at St Mary's and Pendlebury Hospitals, who work unstintingly for the health of sick and premature babies.

Before we turn to the theological understanding which Alex evoked, let me briefly fill out the medical story of his life by four images of him which stay with me. One is seeing him a few days after he was born and wondering at how small he was. (He was so small that his mother borrowed a doll's cardigan from his sister for him to wear.) Another is some months later, holding him, making eye contact and talking to him while he responded by blowing bubbles. Once he did this and tried to smile at the same time – and that is not easy! Another time he did this as I tried to get him to take some baby food. The result was that my spectacles became befogged with what set like cement! Blowing bubbles was a way of responding person-to-person, and he exploited it. A third memory is of approaching him as his mother held him while he sat on a counter at church and being told to hold out my hand to him. He took it; we shook hands. He had learned a new social skill, and we smiled at each other. The final image of him is his smiling response to being noticed, and his gentle touch. His mother mentions his 'special magic': while I do not forget how on one occasion he was arching his back in discomfort, my dominant memory of Alex is of a person who, in his vulnerability, brought a sense of grace and love to those who met him just by who he was.

In what way did Alex affect my understanding? He made me think much more about people who are handicapped. He acted for me as a representative of the many persons who suffer from mental, physical, emotional and spiritual handicaps.

This does not mean that I was not aware of the existence of such people before I met Alex. As a middle-aged, middle-class English university teacher I sometimes indulge myself – particularly in the company of colleagues – in moaning about my situation. Envy leads me to compare myself with those I consider to be more fortunately placed! It does not take me long, however, to see how fortunate I am. I use 'see' deliberately. I do not have to walk far from where I teach to be in a large housing estate which is a social disaster; to pass men and women who wander the streets muttering to themselves while they wait for the night hostel to open; to visit a church drop-in centre where the marginalized and bewildered are offered friendship and guidance in coping with the complexities of modern urban existence; to call on a clinic for physically and emotionally abused children; to attend classes helping children with severe educational problems; to walk past groups of the alienating and the alienated; to enter wards where confused old people sit unresponsively; to visit a Special Care Baby Unit where anxious parents watch while doctors and nurses – with relieving good humour – use disturbing arrays of equipment on their children.

Do not infer from this that I work in an unusually deprived place. It is a typical urban situation. Such people are in all communities. In many cases, however, they seem invisible. Some are 'invisible' because they are hidden away in institutions. (The policy of 'community care', whether it is questionable or commendable as a public policy, will bring more of them into general notice.) Others are invisible because those who care for them are embarrassed to disturb the rest of us by letting us encounter them. They keep them at home and, when they have to go out, successfully shepherd them unnoticed through the streets. Most are invisible because we do not notice. In reflecting on the parable of the good Samaritan, it is easy to criticize the priest and the Levite because the story says that they 'saw' and did not respond. It is also easy to think that when we see the mugged of our society we will respond. What we may not appreciate is how easy it is to pass along the street and not see who is there. We are not deliberately hard-hearted. We just have an ability to shut out from notice that which will disturb us.

What we see or do not see around us is replicated throughout the whole human community. For several years I have been involved with a medium-sized charity. Every half-year the Council has to decide to whom it is to make grants. It is faced with a pile of appeals over a foot high. Most of them are highly worthy. They ask for support for work in caring for the deprived and the handicapped and the unfortunate – from major disaster agencies to local self-help groups. The range of needs that they reflect is enormous. A glance at the *Charities Handbook* will show the range of work in research, prevention and care that is undertaken in and from this country. An intelligent reading of serious newspapers and journals will indicate how much more is needed globally.

What, then, did Alex do for me? He did not make me aware of the existence of handicapped people. If, before he was born, a preacher had accused a congregation of not being aware of them, I would have claimed exemption – although I would not have felt so comfortable if the preacher had gone on to accuse those who were aware of not doing enough for them. But how much is enough? Can there ever be enough?

What, in that case, did Alex do to me that has led me to write this book? He did four things.

Firstly, he heightened my sensitivity to the situations of handicapped people. To use a distinction that Newman makes (1985: 12ff.), what before I had been aware of notionally, I now grasp as a reality. Thought about handicapped people is no longer something that I can do at arm's length. This does not imply that my thought about the issues is so coloured by emotions that it loses its rational balance. What it means is that the issues are no longer abstract matters for me. I now recognize that they refer to real people in real situations.

Whenever I consider such issues, I tend to ask myself, 'What would this mean in practice for a person like Alex?' This is healthy. The criticism that philosophers and theologians live in 'ivory towers' is justified if their ideas are not rooted in the realities of actual life. Alex made certain issues real for me. His story has been outlined so that he may do the same for others. What is going to be discussed in the following chapters is no idealistic theorizing about questions that arise in the course of idle speculations in the comfort of an insulated study. It is about what is actually the case for some people – and about the reality of God's relationship with each and all of us.

Secondly, Alex removed my fear of meeting handicapped people. Perhaps because they remind me of the limits and vulnerability of human being, perhaps because I do not cope easily with unfamiliar situations, perhaps because I am worried about being embarrassed, perhaps because I am impatient, but above all because I did not have the understanding that comes from contact and experience, I used to feel uncomfortable in the presence of handicapped people. As a result of having little to do with them in practice, my basic unease about meeting them probably grew.

Alex changed that. He blew bubbles at me. He smiled. He enjoyed contact with other people, and that included me. His grace removed my fear. His vulnerability called me into relationship. He was a person. And he has become for me a representative person who helps me to approach other handicapped people in the light of my brief encounter with him. Now when I think about handicapped people, it is the fact that they are people rather than that they are handicapped that is dominant. I am no more anxious at the prospect of relationships with them than at the prospect of relationships with other people.

Thirdly, Alex brought me to see the error of judging other people's happiness and fulfilment in terms of what is appropriate for me. We will return to the general issue of the supposed ideal nature and goals of human being in chapter three. Alex showed me the fundamental mistake of being sorry for him just because he could not be expected eventually to do some of the things which I enjoy. He was not like me, and there was no reason to think that he ought to be like me. He was Alex. We were different persons. To respect him meant to recognize this.

Sometimes we place intolerable burdens on our children, pupils, students and junior colleagues because we set before them our unfulfilled ideals for ourselves. We look, generally unconsciously, for satisfaction in their achievement of what

we have not managed to achieve. The other side of this
attitude is that often we feel threatened when they do not
share our values. Lacking confidence in our own worth, their
non-conformity with our pattern of life disturbs us, especially
when it indicates that things we hold dear are in fact among
the non-essential aspects of life. Therefore, instead of enjoying
the rich variety of ways of being human, we want others to
want to be like we want to be. This may not be to love them,
nor even to love the truth as we see it. It may be to love our
own self-image.

This error infects some of the less self-critical forms of
'liberation' theology produced in the First World (and by
Third World theologians who have been seduced into sharing
its values). Both their diagnoses of the social, economic and
political forms of oppression and their specifications of
desirable goals are fundamentally questionable when they
presuppose that the oppressed want – and even more
questionably ought to want – to realize the ideal goals of
First World, middle-class intellectuals! Such a presupposition
is questionable not only because it treats as ideals goals
whose partial realization to date has not suggested the
presence of the kingdom of God on earth. It is also
questionable because it implies that there is a blueprint
which lays out a single pattern for that kingdom.

Alex showed me the error of such attitudes. The recognition
which I came to is summed up by a comment which his
mother made as we talked about this book: 'At first we
looked to see how he would develop; but we came to realize
that he was not developing much. He was; and we enjoyed
what he was.' Alex's worth is not a matter of his having
satisfied some external or internal goals. It is in his having
been himself. And Alex's being himself was not his fulfilment
of anyone's expectations – his own, his parents', his doctors',
or God's. It was to be. The same is true of every person. We
shall return to this issue in chapters five, six and seven.

Fourthly, meeting Alex started me thinking about faith
and theology in relation to handicapped people generally.
While, like every other person, Alex was special and unique,
his being handicapped was not special and unique. There are
many who are handicapped, mentally, emotionally, physically
and spiritually. Some are handicapped from birth, some as a

result of accidents, and some through the processes of disease and aging. What particularly troubled me was the question: What has the Christian gospel to say about the salvation of these people? It is easy, thinking of babies like Alex, to be moved by Jesus' saying, 'Let the children come to me . . . for the kingdom of Heaven belongs to such as these' (Matthew 19.14). What does it mean? What is the saving relationship between God and human beings in the case of people who are classed as being 'handicapped'?

Thinking about Alex has led me to revise my views on the saving reality of God and on the relationship between God and human beings. This revision has not made me give up my earlier criticisms of the models traditionally used in atonement theology. I stand by what I say in 'The Poet of Salvation' about the use of models of ransom, propitiation, vicarious sacrifice, and satisfaction of honour. They are inappropriate to a credible understanding of the divine nature and irrelevant to human self-understanding today. Nor has the revision led me to withdraw the revisionary view of salvation which I maintain in that essay, namely, that the saving activity of God is the twofold activity of preserving what has been experienced and inspiring further expressions of aesthetic value.

Considering how the views expressed in that essay might apply to Alex has, however, made me aware that its understanding of salvation is basically flawed. This is both because of implications which might be drawn from it and because of the essential truth about the divine–human relationship which it overlooks.

The doctrine of salvation which I present there could be interpreted as élitist. It does not show how God's saving activity establishes the significance of the lives of most people. It sees that significance in terms of God as the one who preserves what people have achieved and who inspires them to use what is given in their situation for future creative achievements.

This view of the divinely recognized worth of human beings may seem appropriate in the case of people who have the opportunity and the ability to act creatively. Their feelings, their responses and their actions may be judged to have value such that it is appropriate for God to preserve them in the divine memory. 'Divine inspiration', furthermore, may be understood as what leads them in the future to contribute even more to the wealth of God's all-embracing experience. For these people, then, God may be regarded as 'saviour' according to the revisionary concept of salvation which I put forward. But these people are likely to be envisaged in terms of the Rembrandts and the Shakespeares, the Wordsworths and the Mozarts, the Hegels and the Kierkegaards of the world.

What is worrying about this way of understanding human salvation is that it is in danger of sanctifying the self-regarding attitude of the members of an artistic and intellectual élite who despise 'ordinary people' because they do not share their supposed talents. Has such a view of salvation anything to affirm about the worth of most people? What in these terms is the worth that is contributed to the divine memory by the life of a little girl whose dominant experience before she died was lethargic suffering of hunger and thirst and disease as her family trudged around drought-stricken territory? What is the divine inspiration to further creative achievements that is appropriate to those who pick over rubbish dumps as they struggle to survive in shanty-towns? What novel enrichment of the divine experience is to be looked for from Jack, a single-parent struggling on social security to manage in a society which he finds oppressive, bewildering and unresponsive to his needs? What about homeless Jill who wanders the streets? What about those whose situation leaves them listlessly waiting for nothing and hoping for nothing?

Environment does not determine everything. There are amazing cases of people who respond creatively to their situation. They are exceptions. While some people do not take on the character of the squalor around them, many are crushed by it. They survive indifferently until they die.

And what about the masses of people who live humdrum lives? They do not suffer the dire needs that are highlighted in appeals from charities. Neither do they achieve any particular greatness. There is no deep black nor dazzling white about their lives. Their existence is coloured by indistinct patches of dull greys – and like ships so painted they sail through life unnoticed. What in the divine memory of their lives establishes their worth?

These are some of the worries about my paper that began to arise as I thought about Alex. What had he contributed that established his worth as a remembered part of the divine reality?

As I reflected further on the implications of what I had written in 'The Poet of Salvation', I became aware of a nightmare and of a theological mistake. The nightmare arose from a possible inference from my paper, namely, that a person's worth could be graded according to the richness of his or her contribution to the divine experience. It is on this kind of grading, presumably, that we justify killing vermin and cancerous tumours and bacteria which threaten human lives. Human existence is judged to be more important – to have more value – than that of vermin, tumours and bacteria. My nightmare was that if the worth of human beings depends on the value of what they contribute, some might argue that those who cannot contribute significantly (and even more those whose demands leave them net debtors of value) should be deemed disposable when resources are limited. As I grow older and presumably become more liable to show signs of senility, that is not an argument which I want to endorse! It is, in any case, an invalid argument. The principle behind it is false. Whether value is considered to be quantifiable in monetary or in physical terms, or to be a matter of aesthetic enrichment, a person's significance is not determined by the value of what she or he contributes to others' experiences. Nor does the principle that a person's significance lies in the value of what he or she contributes become valid if God is held to be the ultimate judge and recipient of that value. As will be indicated in chapter five, critical reflection dissolves the nightmare by showing that it is ill-founded.

The theological mistake is that of implying that salvation is something which we affect by our own actions. Superficially it might seem that the understanding of salvation in 'The Poet of Salvation' is properly God-centred. It is God who preserves and it is God who inspires further creative activity. In these respects the essay clearly does not suggest that we *effect* our own salvation: its reality depends on the all-embracing grace of God. At the same time the essay does assert that we significantly *affect* our own salvation – for what God embraces and so becomes everlastingly part of the divine reality is what we produce. In this respect salvation is a matter of human works as well as of divine grace.

The human contribution to salvation is not as dominant in this theological understanding as in a theology which asserts that we (may) earn our acceptance by God through meritorious behaviour. Nevertheless it is at least latent. To hold that the significance of a human being is established by its incorporation in the divine may reasonably be held to imply that the worth of each person is determined by the values which that person produces as she or he contributes to the divine experience. As later discussions will indicate, the issue is a complicated one. God values us as the selves that we are. This means as the selves that our actions determine us to be. On the other hand, what I say in 'The Poet of Salvation' is not satisfactory on its own. The identification of the preserving and inspiring activity of God as saviour needs to be corrected by a prior recognition that we are of worth not because of what we contribute to God but because of the value which God bestows upon us.

The final pages of *God and the Processes of Reality* (Pailin 1989) indicate briefly how my understanding changed. This book is an attempt to do more justice to the insights which Alex brought to me.

The story of changes in my opinions is not important – except perhaps for anyone who has been misled by the élitist anthropocentricity of some ideas in 'The Poet of Salvation'. Is, then, the personal form of this chapter justified? It may be: a knowledge of how it all began may help readers to understand what follows.

One final comment: Alex brought insights to me for which I am grateful. If some – indeed, if all – of those insights are mistaken, do not blame Alex! He brought grace.

2

From a theology of handicap to a theology of human being

The previous chapter describes how a brief encounter with Alex raised questions about the character of salvation and the significance of human being. As Herbert of Cherbury emphasizes, God is the 'Creator, Redeemer, and Preserver' to whom all may turn, whatever their 'condition' and whatever their cultural and religious backgrounds (Herbert of Cherbury 1886: 60). Only as God is so envisaged is the universality which is an essential characteristic of divine providence properly recognized (cf. Herbert of Cherbury 1937: 291; 1705: *passim*). An understanding of faith in God which does not make sense of the lives of all people thereby shows itself to be mistaken.

Meeting Alex not only made me revise my understanding of salvation to remove possible élitist implications. It also provoked me to explore the notion of what I initially called 'a handicapped theology'. Since, however, that title might tempt critics to describe what eventually emerged as 'a very handicapped theology', I soon changed it to 'a theology of handicap'!

Implicit in this choice of a title was the idea that the project would consider a particular form of 'liberation theology'. It would be parallel to such other forms as 'feminist theology', 'black theology' and 'political theology'. This view of the project was partly the result of a conversation with a student. She was proposing to investigate how the ideas of some liberation theologians apply to life in a British city today. As we discussed the topics involved in such a thesis, she pointed to a gap in the literature. There seemed to be no 'liberation theology' for one group of disadvantaged people – those who are handicapped.

Her comment echoed concerns which Alex had aroused in me. It seemed that what I proposed to investigate would help

15

to plug that gap. As I thought further about the project,
however, I discovered that the idea of writing a *liberation*
theology of handicap was mistaken on two counts. Firstly,
whatever might eventually emerge would differ from
liberation theologies in basic respects. Secondly, handicap
does not pose the theological problem that it is commonly –
and superficially – thought to pose. What is needed is not a
theology concerned with the handicapped as a distinct group
of people, but a theology of the human as such which takes
account of the 'handicapped' state of some people and clearly
recognizes them as part of humankind. In this chapter we
shall consider the reasons for these two conclusions.

What is a 'liberation theology'? It is an attempt to discover,
predominantly in practical terms, what the 'good news' of
salvation means now for people who are identified as
oppressed and disadvantaged. According to Letty Russell:

> Liberation theology brings into focus the Biblical message
> of God's Mission to set humankind free from bondage. In
> the light of oppression experienced by Third World people
> and women, it seeks to tell the good news of liberation in
> such a way that people can hear, understand, and accept
> this message of God's gift of freedom and salvation in their
> lives. The 'cantus firmus of the liberating message' of the
> Bible is the good news (*basar*) of deliverance experienced
> by the Hebrew people, and the good news (*euangelion*) of
> the establishment of God's rulership as experienced by the
> early followers of Jesus Christ (Isaiah 52:7; Matthew 4:17).

The different types of liberation theology use the formative
stories of the Christian faith to identify the way to freedom
and justice today. The 'good news' of the gospel is thus made
relevant to 'the present experience and future hope' of people
who want 'liberation *now*' (Russell 1974: 104).

Liberation theology is not restricted to the two cases
mentioned by Russell – the situation of people in the Third
World and women. Its concern to identify the significance
and especially the practical implications of believing the
gospel extends to all who are oppressed and disadvantaged.
Liberation theologians thus explore the relevance of faith to
what is happening politically, economically, socially and

culturally in various parts of the world. Their concerns include global ecological issues, since the destruction of the natural environment threatens the welfare of everyone.

Faith in God is not (at least, is not simply or even mainly) a matter of '"pi" in the sky when you die' – whether the 'pi' be the piety of the beatific vision or the pie of a heavenly feast. The doctrine of God as creator and the belief that God incorporates each experience within Godself imply that what happens in the world is significant for God. As such it must also be important to those who believe in God. The prophets of ancient Israel perceived that God is not to be fobbed off with savoury smells. Obedience to God involves social justice. From its beginning the Christian community has considered that faith's authenticity is falsified by the absence of realistic help for others (James 2.14ff; 1 John 4.19ff). Belief in God as loving and love for the neighbour cannot be separated – and the class of 'neighbour' has no bounds. The parables of the good Samaritan and of the sheep and goats (Luke 10.29ff; Matthew 25.31ff) have imprinted this on Christian consciousness.

In the past this aspect of faith was predominantly considered in terms of care given to individuals by individuals. It was as individuals that those in need were perceived as asking for and being given friendship, food, shelter, sanctuary, medical care and education. And even if the assistance was provided in many cases by charitable institutions rather than in the form of this individual giver to that individual recipient, those institutions were justifiably regarded as ways of mediating gifts from individual benefactors. This was an understandable view of love in action. It is Betty and Arthur who are lonely, homeless, hungry, cold, threatened, ill and uneducated, not some abstract class of 'people in need'. To be concerned about people generally can be a way of avoiding caring for anyone in particular.

In recent decades this understanding of Christian love has been modified. Marxist analyses have helped theologians to recognize the extent to which the needs of individuals are the result of the situations in which they find themselves. While acts of benevolence will ease their position, the quality of life that is properly to be desired for everyone will only become possible for them when the factors which create those needs are changed. Such changes require political, economic, social, cultural and ecological action. The different liberation theologies are the product of the combination of this recognition with Enlightenment assumptions about the rights of people to corporate and individual autonomy and Christian convictions about the love of God and the worth of each person.

Some liberation theologies focus attention on the need for political justice. They expose regimes by which people are oppressed and consider how just structures may be established. Their goal is freedom for people in corporate groups (however the boundaries of those groups be determined) to control their own affairs while paying due regard to the rights of individuals and minorities within them. Other liberation theologies investigate how the economically weak may resist exploitation by the powerful. The liberation which they seek is that which comes from a fair and sustainable distribution of the world's resources.

A third form of liberation theology is concerned with freedom from social forms of oppression, most notably those based on sex and race. Women are made conscious of the ways in which social structures and attitudes place barriers across the route of their development as human beings. Racial groups protest about the discrimination from which they suffer. Liberation here is freedom to enjoy full personhood.

Some liberation theologies focus attention on culture. They protest against imperialist expansionism in ways of thought and practice, highlighting the danger that the mass media, through the global coverage which is now possible, will obliterate rather than enrich cultural diversity. They affirm the freedom to be different and to cherish differences – the freedom to grow many varieties of apple in spite of the desire for uniformity among supranational bureaucrats! They promote freedom to have Chinese as well as European forms of music, to be challenged by Cage as well as by Mozart, by Mondrian as well as by Rubens, by Beckett as well as by Sophocles, by haikus as well as by sonnets, by stories of the Dream-time as well as of the patriarchs.

Ecological forms of liberation theology focus attention on dangers to the environment from inadequately controlled industrial, agricultural, commercial and domestic activities. Earlier concerns about 'the silent spring' and the exhaustion of natural resources have been joined by warnings about the 'greenhouse' effect, the depletion of the ozone layer, the destruction of the rain forests and pollution by industrial waste. Liberation here is freedom for people to live in a safe and richly varied world, a freedom in which the needs of all its inhabitants are met in a world-sustaining manner.

These different forms of liberation theology raise many questions. What is justice? Who decides? How far should individual liberty be restricted by the welfare of the community? What is responsible political freedom? How are the needs for food and shelter to be balanced against the dangers of chemical pollution by pesticides and the destruction of the environment to provide materials for housing?

Some liberation theologies have been unrealistic. Images have been presented of a society that could only exist if the world was essentially other than it is. A student once told me that the only way forward was to ban procreation globally for forty years! This would reduce the world's population to a size where his ideals for human existence could be realized. It was sad that he did not find his plan for the way forward a *reductio ad absurdum* of his policy.

Not only have some liberation theologies failed to perceive the complexities of practical policies, they have also been naively optimistic about people. Theological doctrines about original sin and Hobbes' description of human existence in the state of nature (i.e., of uncontrolled freedom) as 'solitary, poor, nasty, brutish, and short' (Hobbes: 82) may not be delightful, but they draw attention to characteristics which liberation theologies ignore at the cost of credibility. There is no guarantee that people who are freed from one unjust situation will not create another. The inhabitants of ancient Jericho would have had good reason not to blow trumpets of joy at the appearance of freed slaves from Egypt (cf. Joshua 6). Liberation for one group is perverse when it results in the destruction of another. Mary Daly, for instance, criticizes some 'black' liberation theologies on the grounds that so far as women are concerned they promote only 'a pigmentation operation'; they do not remove the offence of patriarchal behaviour (cf. Daly 1973: 25).

Nevertheless, however unrealistic some liberation theologies may be – and *some* does not mean *all* – they are motivated by an important insight into the implications of faith in God. Applying the gospel to what happens, they consider what it means for those who are oppressed and disadvantaged and how 'a more humane society' may be created in which all persons are 'full participants' (Russell 1974: 20).

Bearing in mind the principles of liberation theology, it seemed to me appropriate to try to develop a liberation theology for handicapped people. The description 'handicapped' indicates that such people are regarded as disadvantaged even if they are not positively oppressed – and in the competitive structures of society their disadvantages may well result, albeit unintentionally, in them feeling, and in some cases being, oppressed. The basic question of a liberation theology for handicapped people appeared to be: How is the gospel to be applied to the situation of such people so that it frees them from the injustice of failures to recognize their dignity as human beings, of obstacles to their full development as persons, and of hindrances to their full participation in society? Furthermore, while the investigation was intended to be relevant to all types of handicap, it was to be particularly concerned with those whose handicaps seem to others to inhibit severely their capacity for creative, autonomous living.

Reflection on this basic question, however, showed that what would emerge as a theology of handicap would not (and, by its nature, could not) satisfy some of the basic principles advocated by liberation theologians. Should it, therefore, be regarded as a form of 'liberation theology'?

In the first place, a number of liberation theologians maintain that the oppressed must be encouraged to speak for themselves. This is partly on the grounds that outsiders do not share the definitive experiences of the oppressed and accordingly may not fully understand their situation. No matter how imaginative their empathy, the fact that they are outsiders means that they cannot, for example, share the oppressed's sense of being trapped. Hence some feminist, black and political liberation theologians argue that because only those who are women, black and live under totalitarian regimes can fully appreciate what it is to be in those situations, only they have the insights as well as the right to suggest what should be done to remedy them.

The limitations of empathy are, however, debatable. The fact that I am male, white and do not live under a blatantly unjust regime cannot fail to influence my judgements – and probably much more than I am aware. For there to be accurate and adequate discussions, it is important that, so far as it is possible, the disadvantaged should be encouraged to identify and reflect on their situation. Nevertheless, while those who are not disadvantaged may achieve only a partial sense of how the disadvantaged experience life, it does not follow that all their attempts to appreciate the conditions of others are worthless.

Another argument against comment by outsiders is more compelling. This maintains that part of the dignity of being a liberated person is to have and to exercise the right 'to be an active *subject* of historical change, and not merely its passive *object*' (Ogden 1989: 21f). To have this right includes, among other things, to have the right to speak for oneself. The title of the radio programme *Does He Take Sugar?* points to the dehumanizing – as well as discourteous – way in which the disadvantaged are often not given the opportunity to express their own preferences. Consequently some liberation theologies draw attention to the importance of the report about naming in the creation story (Genesis 2.19f): it indicates that to be a human being is to have power to determine the significance of the environment. Others echo Kant's view that those who have come 'of age' ought no longer to accept the direction of 'guardians'. The motto of 'enlightenment' is *'Sapere aude!* – Have courage to use your own reason!' The liberated, like the enlightened, must use their understanding 'without direction from another' (cf. Kant 1959: 85). A 'liberation theology' which speaks from the outside is thus in danger of contradicting itself. The advocates of liberation must take care not to become new guardians who patronizingly inform the disadvantaged what is their 'real' condition and what they should do about it. Otherwise conscientization (or consciousness-raising) becomes a high-principled term for a new form of controlling and demeaning indoctrination.

It is not, therefore, primarily for the sake of accurate information that the disadvantaged must be encouraged to speak about their conditions and their hopes. An essential characteristic of liberation is that the unfree realize their freedom to speak for themselves.

In the case of many mentally and a few physically handicapped people, however, this principle of liberation theology has very limited application. Their condition is such that while they certainly have feelings and preferences that ought to be respected, they apparently understand situations only to a limited extent; and they are severely restricted in their ability to communicate what they do feel and understand. Accordingly, whatever their views and feelings may be, they can only be disclosed if others find ways to express them on their behalf.

This dependence upon the empathy and insights of others indicates the enormous vulnerability of many handicapped people. They are always in danger of having their own understanding distorted or ignored as others take it upon themselves, from a self-affirming 'superior' position, to decide what they ought to want and what in any case is in their best interests. It is easy to be blinkered in this respect.

I was amused to listen to a conversation between two parents. They complained bitterly about doctors who had not bothered to consult them, let alone talk to their children, before deciding upon some treatment for those children. 'Who do they think we are? Aren't the children's feelings important?' Their protests seemed appropriate. And yet within five minutes their discussion had moved on to what they were 'going to have to do' with their own aged parents. One seemed oblivious to the possibility that her father might have views on the matter; the other dismissed his parents' preferences as embarassingly silly – 'They just don't know what is really good for them'! From some standpoints the latter judgement might have been warranted – and, as is illustrated by the gap between advice and practice in matters of eating, drinking, and exercise, it is not only the young and the aged who perversely choose to do what, by certain objective criteria, is not in their best interests! Unhappily the parents' feelings and autonomy seemed to be regarded as stupidity to be got around rather than wishes to be considered seriously. The condition of those who cannot express their preferences clearly, and even more of those who have difficulty in becoming aware of what they prefer, is much less happy. It is only too easy to decide for them.

No matter how caring others may intend to be, their actions are thus in danger of dehumanizing those whom they seek to represent. The feelings, insights and desires of handicapped people themselves must be taken seriously. On the other hand, in the case of many handicapped people, particularly those who have the greatest problems in understanding and communicating, what else can be done but to try to be sensitive to their dignity and to speak for them? The way in which some people are handicapped means that their insights and desires are formed by a limited perception of the situation and are inadequately expressed. As inheritors of the Enlightenment we may resent being told to trust experts just as much as children do not like being told, 'Your parents know best.' Nevertheless, in certain situations it seems that nothing better is possible. Some people have significantly deeper insights than others into what is happening and into what can and should be done about it.

A liberation theology for some handicapped people is, therefore, only possible if others take it upon themselves to speak for those who are to be 'liberated'. Such people have a difficult balancing act. On the one hand they must respect the understanding and wishes of those whom they seek to represent. They must try to avoid a patronizing imposition of their own ideas. On the other hand they must accept that in some cases those wishes may not only be impractical or distorted; they may also be based on an inadequate appreciation of the situation. While, therefore, handicapped people must be strongly encouraged to produce their own liberation theologies, in some cases – and particularly in the kind of case that provoked this study – those theologies can only emerge by others doing it with and to a large degree for such people.

A second, related difference between some liberation theologies and what I initially mooted as a 'liberation theology of the handicapped' concerns the desirability of separate development. According to a number of liberation theologies the members of an oppressed group must not only take up their right to name their experiences and to think through for themselves what they want. They must also be permitted, even encouraged, to work out their own pattern of authentic life in their own communities without, as far as possible, interference by others.

This demand is justified to some extent in some cases. People who have been subjected to racial, religious, national or sexual prejudice may cease to feel threatened when they are in the company of others who share their characteristics. There they can explore the nature of their personhood without pressure to conform to the norms of those who have previously discriminated against them. The oppressed may thus find it easiest to discover their dignity in the company of those who have similarly suffered.

Some black liberation theologians have accordingly called for 'blacks' to band together in their own communities in order to discover how 'black is beautiful' and to gain confidence to affirm their place as full members of the human community. In a parallel way some feminist thinkers have urged women to unite in groups where they will be able to support each other in developing their personhood without feeling obliged to 'prove' themselves to male members of society by satisfying standards which males have laid down.

Such 'apartheid' policies may be defensible in some cases as temporary procedures which prepare the unfree to exercise their liberty. They are not defensible as the basis of permanent states within society – unless it can be shown that since the human community is composed of ineradicable groups, it must be permanently divided in order to prevent some groups of people oppressing others.

To divide up humanity is to reduce the potential richness of life for every person and for every group. The point of liberation is to free each person to attain the fullest satisfaction. This is only possible if each person is freed to belong to a community in which all are included. In this way liberation enriches the possibilities for the oppressor as well as for the oppressed.

What, in that case, should be the preferred situation in society of those whose handicaps have marginalized them? They may find it easier to affirm their worth as persons by living with others who mostly share their disadvantages rather than in the company of those who are predominantly without such handicaps. Hence communities in which handicapped people can live and work together have been established. They are intended to provide their inhabitants with an atmosphere of positive acceptance which they may not find in the stressed situations of society generally.

These communities may offer considerable satisfaction to their members. Those who question their establishment must consider whether there is a better way to promote the personal development of some of those who are handicapped. What is called 'community care' in a society dominated by competition and 'market forces' may be a way of using high-sounding ideals as an excuse for abandoning those who need support to situations with which they cannot cope.

Nevertheless, is there a better way than such an 'apartheid' solution to meet the needs of handicapped people? In certain cases it seems that the answer to the question is that there is not. A few people are so limited or disturbed that they have to be restricted for their own sake. Some lack the minimum bodily co-ordination needed to care for themselves; some lack the mental awareness to protect themselves. If they are not to be destroyed by self-neglect and avoidable harm, they have to live in places where others can ensure their physical well-being. In other cases such a solution may be warranted as a necessary *but temporary* way by which handicapped people can develop the skills necessary for living in the community at large.

As a general policy for most handicapped people for most of the time, however, an 'apartheid' solution is far from obviously appropriate. Although the tactical use of such a policy advocated by some black and feminist theologians may be justified as a temporary expedient, in the case of handicapped people generally such a tactic can never be regarded as a temporary expedient to enable the fundamental problem facing the group to be removed. As will shortly be discussed, handicapped people generally stay handicapped. In most cases to attempt to implement liberation for them by a policy of separate development, however appropriate it may be in other forms of liberation theology, is to prevent them taking their place in the human community and to deprive that community of some of its members.

This is not acceptable. Handicapped people are persons. As part of the human community they are not to be separated from it. Their inclusion in the community of all liberates all of us from prejudice and ignorance that limit our own personhood.

Recognition of this principle, however, must not be allowed to become a way by which members of the community ignore the demands that the needs of handicapped persons place upon them. Mary Daly protests at the way in which liberation for women is evaded by universalizing the issue (cf. Daly 1973: 5). Apparently sympathetic listeners respond to the demand to end discrimination against women by advocating the policy that *all* forms of discrimination should be ended. This general policy, however, tends to act as a shield against pressure to become involved in eradicating any particular form of discrimination.

While, therefore, handicapped people are to be incorporated as far as possible as members of the community, they must also be recognized to have special needs and hence to require special consideration if society is to be fair to all its members. Although the fact that resources are finite means that it is not possible for society to meet all the legitimate needs of its members (for example, it is regrettably the case that it would destroy society if it tried to finance all the medical care that is technically possible and wanted), much more is possible within even tolerable limits than is at present provided. Buildings and vehicles need to be designed so that physically handicapped people can have access to them. Attitudes and values need to be rethought to take account of the satisfaction of mentally handicapped persons. It is not enough to say that they are free to participate so far as they can. That can be like telling a blind and deaf couple that they are free to go to the opera at Glyndebourne if they can afford it. Just as liberation for handicapped people does not mean imposing on them separate development, so too it does not mean ignoring the need for special action to help them to develop as members of the community.

Liberation theologies differ from a theology of handicap, thirdly, in that the former have a basic goal which is inappropriate for the latter. In general liberation theologies look to the establishment of a state of freedom from which the structures that prevent people realizing their fullest potentialities have been eradicated (cf. Ogden 1989: 103). Their aim is rather like that of doctors treating an epidemic: successful treatment means that the disease disappears. Political liberation theology thus looks to the realization of social orders in which all members of the community participate and in which none are unjustifiably prevented from expressing themselves. Liberation theologies for women and for blacks do not, of course, attempt to destroy sex and race. What they aim to destroy are social attitudes and practices that unfairly discriminate between people on the basis of those characteristics. If – would that it were appropriate to say *when* – they succeed, a person's sex and race will be as irrelevant to their social situation as whether there is an odd number of letters in their surname.

The case of handicapped people is different. Reformation of social attitudes could alter their situation in important respects. In place of the marginalization that is often their lot, they would come to receive the consideration due to any person just because she or he is a person. Instead of being excluded, positive discrimination could ensure that they are included. Nevertheless, any policy of inclusion would have to be qualified by an ineradicable 'wherever possible'. Liberation could never eradicate their identifying disadvantage – that they are handicapped.

A group of young people, for example, may make great efforts to ensure that one of their members is bumped along in her wheelchair when they hike in the hills. But no matter how vigorous their refusal to let her be excluded, they cannot override the fact that they have the freedom to scramble unaided up rock faces while she has not and never will have that possibility. A blind person will never share my delight at the colours of a painting by Turner, nor a deaf person the subtle harmonies of Mozart. The goodwill of a family to incorporate a mentally handicapped man in their conversations cannot limit their discussions to topics in which he can participate without denying the development of their own interests. On some issues he cannot share their thinking. Nor, if a woman is severely handicapped, will she be able to control her own pattern of life by exercising many of the freedoms (and sharing the anxieties) taken for granted by non-handicapped people.

To the extent that the handicaps of some people are due to their natural constitution, the goal of total liberation for them is a delusion. Social, political and economic engineering will not stop them being handicapped. In this respect, a theology of the handicapped cannot share the vision – and goal – of a liberated state where all will be well, at least not in the sense that handicap will have been eradicated together with political oppression, social discrimination and economic injustice.

On the other hand, because forms of handicap cannot be ended, it does not follow that nothing should be done to help those who are handicapped. To draw such a conclusion is as morally mistaken as for a doctor to hold that because she cannot cure a patient, she need not do anything to ease his suffering. The obligation to care is, furthermore, not one which individuals can hand over to the community, nor the community to individuals. Action is required at all levels. The 'welfare state mentality' of post-war decades may have tempted some individuals to consider that the proper needs of people can and should be met by 'the state'. The political doctrines of the 'new right' which have been promoted in recent years may tempt others to hold that those responsible for the affairs of state should hand over welfare responsibilities to individuals (parents must care for their handicapped children, children must care for their senile parents) and to voluntary charitable organizations, including the churches, which are dependent on individuals giving them money and time.

The odium that has attached itself to Pilate for washing his hands of a nasty problem should be a warning to those who today seek to shirk responsibility for ensuring that whatever is appropriate is done to give handicapped people opportunities for a satisfyingly fulfilling life. This requires *both* corporate *and* individual action. Pilate may be defended for acting prudently as a governor who wished to avoid imposing an alien's judgement on a restless community split by baffling religious squabbles. There is no such defence for failing to help handicapped people. Voters who want to cut taxes, politicians who want power while avoiding responsibility in Whitehall-protected ignorance, groups who want self-centredly to enjoy their own pleasures, and individuals who want an easy life may try to evade the uncomfortable demands of responding to the needs of handicapped people. The more they succeed, the more they are the proper objects of the obloquy directed at the Pilate of caricature.

The fact that the demands of care can never be finally satisfied is no excuse for failing to respond to the needs of handicapped people. The boy scout who misunderstood his promise as one 'to do a good turn to everyone some day', and so considered that he need not do anything for anyone on any particular day, fell for a hermeneutical confusion which many seem to share. Jesus may have said, 'You have the poor among you always' (Matthew 26.11; John 12.8), but he also, according to the gospel records, condemned those who fail to care for those in need (cf. Matthew 25.31–46).

Nevertheless, while it is important to ensure that the handicapped (as all others) enjoy the dignity and quality of life which is the proper goal for each person, it also has to be admitted that the handicapped will never be liberated from their handicaps. Unlike liberation theologies, a theology of handicap cannot hope to secure the eradication of the condition which identifies handicapped people as such. In this respect, too, a theology of handicap is significantly different from liberation theologies.

A fourth and fundamental difference between liberation theologies and a theology of handicap emerges when attempts are made to define the referent of the description 'handicapped people'. Consideration of this issue not only further highlights the questionableness of classing a theology of handicap as a liberation theology, it also reveals that the notion of 'theology of handicap' itself is fundamentally unsatisfactory. Why is this?

The basic problem is the notion of 'handicap'. It cannot be

defined, even loosely, without implying a standard of comparison. If this standard is based on a notion of what is normative for human being, it is unwarrantable. In the remainder of this chapter we will briefly consider why this is so, and why the supposed problem of a theology of handicap turns out to be a problem of the theology of human being.

From the beginning my proposal to investigate 'a theology of handicap' intended the description 'handicap' very broadly. This was deliberate, even though the usage could be criticized on the grounds that to consider so broad a range of conditions under one label was liable to obscure important distinctions.

This criticism makes an important point. There are different kinds and degrees of handicap. For many purposes they need to be treated separately. Mental handicap is different from physical, and these from emotional handicap. Although they are less noticed, there are also what may be called aesthetic, moral and spiritual handicaps: some people lack the capacity to appreciate forms of beauty, or to recognize the categorical imperative of morality, or to have a sense of wonder, or to be aware of the sacred, the holy, the numinous.

Since there are different types of handicap, it is important to recognize that the fact that a person has one handicap does not mean that she or he must also be handicapped in other ways. Van Gogh's mental instability did not prevent him producing great art. His turmoil may even have contributed to the visions of reality which he made available for others through his paintings. That a person is physically uncoordinated implies nothing about their mental, moral and aesthetic sensitivity. A distinguished philosopher once told me that he was turned down for military service because at the medical examination he was asked to shut his eyes and hop from one corner of the room to another. He tried, but he could not do it! This lack of coordination, however, had no effect on his philosophical insights – nor on his enjoyment of exhausting (for his guests) walks in the hills. For over twenty years Stephen Hawking has been confined to a wheelchair by motor neuron disease, but his theories about the cosmos, and especially about its first moments, place him at the forefront of theoretical physicists in the world.

Each of the major kinds of handicap, furthermore, covers a range of forms that it is often important to distinguish. In the case of mental handicap, for instance, those with learning difficulties face very different problems from those who are unable to enter into satisfactory social relationships, and those who have never had certain intellectual powers from those who are to some degree conscious that they have lost them. Within the class of emotional handicaps, it is important in certain contexts to recognize the differences between lacking the capacity for feelings, being incapable of admitting to having feelings, suffering from the black dog of depression, and being unable to temper manic enthusiasms. Physical handicap too has many forms. People may be blind, dumb, deaf, uncoordinated; they may have defective organs or be without certain limbs; they may suffer from progressive deterioration in their organs.

Those who have a handicap in common may, however, have it to markedly different degrees. Learning difficulties, for instance, may range from the need for remedial help with spelling to problems with understanding simple sentences. Physical handicap varies from manual clumsiness to massive paralysis. The causes of handicap also vary. Some are congenital, some due to disease, some the result of accident, some the consequence of human action, and some part of the normal processes of human existence. For many purposes, therefore, and particularly in relation to practical responses, the differences between forms of handicap need to be acknowledged. To fail to do this is to fail to give handicapped persons the dignity that belongs to them as individuals.

Nevertheless, however justified the criticism that a broad use of the term 'handicap' obscures important distinctions, it seemed at first obvious to reply that whatever the character, causes and degrees of their disabilities, all handicapped people have this in common – that they suffer from some form of handicap. The broad use of the term thus appeared to be defensible against the charge of promoting linguistically derived confusion.

The cogency of this reply starts to unravel when attempts are made to define who are the handicapped and, in particular, to decide how they are to be identified as distinct from the non-handicapped. The description of someone as 'handicapped' finds its root meaning in the notion of a disadvantage or hindrance suffered by or imposed upon a competitor in a race. In relation to other competitors some may be 'handicapped' because they are suffering from jet-lag or an illness or because they are made to carry weights or to start further from the finish. Applied generally, as when we talk of 'the handicapped' without reference to a particular competition, the description may be metaphorical but it implies that life is to be understood as a competition with others and that those so describable are impeded in meeting the challenges of that competition.

This understanding of life is questionable. It is not self-evident that human existence must be regarded as essentially a competition – even though physical existence requires a certain degree of success in securing resources from a limited supply. Although human beings may consider themselves subject to a moral demand that they realize their potentials, and although Christians are called to be perfect (cf. Matthew 5.48), it is a mistake (even if a widespread mistake) to interpret these obligations in terms of a command to struggle against others. To live is not to be thrust into an Olympics of life where only a few can get medals and where some people are severely handicapped in the competitions for them.

So far as it is justifiable to consider that individuals, just because they live, are essentially in competition, it should be restricted to thinking of them as being in competition with themselves – in a kind of private competition to fulfil their individual potentials. What is important in that case is not that a person is better or worse than other people at a particular skill, but that she or he enjoys what she or he is capable of to the full. And in this respect it may well be that many of those described as handicapped fulfil far more of their potential than people generally who, with greater ranges of possibility, succumb to the temptation to be satisfied with lower rates of realization. As Jesus pointed out, the widow's mite is worth more than the wealthy's largess because it represents all she has (cf. Mark 12.41–4). Alex's achievement in managing – once – to sit up by himself is on the scale of intrinsic value vastly greater than, say, my climbing Tryfan in Snowdonia.

The fundamental error in regarding life as a competition in which some are disadvantaged is not, however, because it treats individuals as rivals. The fundamental error is in presuming that there is an identifiable norm for human being which all must seek to satisfy and against which all can be judged. The recognition of a common norm is, of course, a prerequisite of a fair competition: all taking part must know by what standard (e.g., speed over the distance, height cleared, weight achieved) the competitors are to be graded. There is, in contrast, no universal standard of human being against which all persons can be measured and by which they can be ranked.

It may be objected that this is not so for Christians. According to their faith Jesus constitutes such a standard for all people. Those who make this response, however, must make it clear in what concrete respects he acts as that standard. Is it in caring for others, in being an itinerant, in his trust in God's guidance and his obedience to what he considered to be his divine calling, in being a miracle-worker, in being a critic of the religious establishment, in not supporting himself, in dividing families, in being non-conformist, in being a provocative teacher, in being unmarried, in . . . ? Furthermore, they must show how the answer to this question is to be determined. Formally all Christians may confess that Jesus is the perfect example of human being; profound problems arise when they attempt to define what this means in material terms. In practice the figure of Jesus drawn from the gospel records is largely made to conform to the understanding of human being entertained by those presenting him as the standard.

In a paper which applies insights arising from feminist critiques of masculine imperialism to attitudes towards other religions, Marjorie Suchocki points out that the result of universalizing a set of material characteristics as an absolute norm for human being is doubly mistaken. It may unjustifiably oppress those who are judged not to satisfy the norm and distort the self-understanding of those who do satisfy it by obscuring the particularity of the norm. According to Suchocki, the proper goal for human liberation, whether in relations between the sexes or in relations between faiths, is that of 'justice' – where 'justice' is understood in formal terms as 'inclusiveness of well-being'. It is realized in a mutually enriching recognition of material diversity (cf. Suchocki 1987: 154; cf. 150ff).

Suchocki's thesis may be universalized. It applies to human being as such. There is no single set of material values which define what it is to be fully and properly human. Those who seek to lay down such a norm are imposing a bureaucratic ideal of standardization which corresponds more to the dullness of bulk manufacture than to the exciting richness characteristic of creativity. From this two conclusions follow. Firstly, because there are no universal standards by which to judge success or estimate handicap, the notion of human being as a competition against others is mistaken. Secondly, for the same reason, there is no universal way of identifying what is meant by 'handicap'.

Like the description 'radical' today (and 'deist' in the eighteenth century), the connotation of the term 'handicapped', when used to describe a person, depends upon who is using it. It indicates that the person so described lacks something which the describer regards as important. There is no reason to suppose that the person so described shares that sense of lack nor, even more importantly, that they ought to share it. Individuals are different. To use standards which one group finds important as a basis for judging all others may be an act of unjustified imperialism.

What is happening when the sighted feel sorry for the blind, the hearing for the deaf, those who can sing in tune for those who cannot, those who enjoy climbing for those with vertigo, those who are intrigued by philosophical puzzles for those who fail to see the problems, those who like red wine for those who get migraine from drinking it, and so on? Those who are sorry are in effect saying of the others, 'It is a pity that you cannot share experiences which I value. As a result your life appears to me handicapped.'

This seems a straightforward way of responding to those who are handicapped. We find some things so important for our lives that there is nothing wrong or condescending in wishing that others could enjoy them. This desire may indeed be regarded as an essential part of the love that constitutes authentic human being. Some, of course, may not wish to share these experiences; if so, that is their privilege as autonomous persons. Others, however, *cannot* share them; they are those whom we consider to be handicapped. As we compare ourselves with these people, we consider ourselves fortunate. Certain experiences are possible for us but not for them. This does not mean that whenever we attempt to help the handicapped we must be acting out of a sense of superiority or even out of an unwarranted sense of guilt about our good luck. While such considerations may sometimes motivate conduct in such cases, generally – and creditably – people seek to help the handicapped simply because they are sensible of their own good fortune and wish to share it with those not so fortunate.

Since such a response seems so appropriate and justified, it is surprising to discover that in one respect at least it may be considered to be a questionable response. What is questionable about it emerges when it is universalized. If any person who is unable to share experiences, skills and delights that another finds important may be regarded as more or less handicapped, and hence as an object of pity, the only one who can conceivably not be so pitied is God. God alone is the one whose experience embraces the experiences of all others and whose being lacks no good quality. Human beings, in contrast, are finite. To be sorry for all those who lack things enjoyed by others may thus be to be sorry that they are not God. If, therefore, to designate people as handicapped is not for us to play God by using our own perceived qualities as the norm for human being, it may in a subtle way be for us to condemn them for not being God – and to fail to appreciate that we too are under the same condemnation.

Alex was limited in what he could do. But so is each of us. As we shall consider in later chapters, what is fundamentally important about each of us is that we *are*, not what we have done nor what we are capable of doing. The concept of 'handicap' as such is as significant or insignificant as that of 'finite' as a description of human being.

In response to the claim that the description 'handicapped' is generally applicable to human beings as such, it may be argued that while all persons are finite, the description 'handicapped' is a justifiable way of distinguishing persons whose abilities and opportunities are notably limited in comparison with those of people generally. It is in this sense, often with the qualifier 'severely' to emphasize the condition being considered, that the term is primarily intended in this study. It is important to note, however, that this understanding of the description 'handicapped' does not identify a class of persons which is separate from others when the whole life of a person – any person – is considered. Whatever may be the autonomy of some mature human beings, everyone begins life in a dependent and restricted state. We live because others cared for us. We develop as persons as and because others respond to us. Without care and response we would not merely be stunted – 'handicapped' – in our development. We would not survive. Furthermore, the state of massive dependency which characterizes the initial period of life is one to which many of us will return to some degree as we enter old age. The lack of autonomy which may seem to identify Alex as a handicapped person and thereby distinguish him from other 'non-handicapped' persons is characteristic of every person to some extent at every stage of their existence, and massively at some stages. Reflection on the nature of human being thus further indicates the broad applicability of the description 'handicapped'.

What, then, was conceived as a liberation theology for handicapped people turns out to be something different. Not only does the project fail to satisfy the principles of self-expression, separate development and eradication appropriate to liberation theology, it also fundamentally fails to identify a distinct group of people who are to be the object of its concern. To ask about the significance of life in relation to handicapped people is to ask about the significance of life for every human being. All are limited. All begin and many end life in a state of massive dependence, whatever may be the possibilities of creative autonomy available to them in between. What began, therefore, as an investigation into the theology of handicap posed by a brief encounter with Alex, and was initially intended to be concerned with the notions of worth and divine salvation for people similarly handicapped, turns out to be a theology of human being as such. Those we call the handicapped, and particularly those we regard as severely handicapped, highlight the vulnerability and questionableness of all human existence.

Nevertheless, it is useful to focus attention on those we

distinguish – confusedly and ultimately unjustifiably – as being 'handicapped'. By considering their human existence we are brought to ask questions and seek answers concerning the significance of human being which, in our pride and prejudice, we prefer to ignore. Those we think of as handicapped help us to gain insight into fundamental truths about ourselves and about God's saving response to us. Therefore, in spite of reservations about its usefulness as a mode of identification, the description 'handicapped' will continue to be used in this study because it confronts us in a powerful way with the finitude and limitations of all human being.

What is true for Alex is true for each of us as human beings. What cannot be true for Alex cannot be true of God's saving relationship to any of us if God is correctly symbolized as the caring parent of all humankind. Accordingly Alex is not to be marginalized as a member of the class of those whom we distinguish from ourselves on the grounds that they are 'handicapped' persons. Alex represents each of us. The significance of his human being before God is the significance of each of us. What this significance is and how it is to be expressed in the community of humankind is the issue which we are now to address.

3

What is the problem?

If, as was suggested in the previous chapter, a theology of handicap is not a liberation theology, and if every person, because of the nature of human being, may be described as handicapped to some extent, does Alex bring to our attention a genuine problem for theological understanding? If so, what is it? Or is the problem which he represents a practical and pastoral one (though not any the less an important problem), namely, the problem of how to ensure that people like him are enabled to enjoy life to the fullest possible extent and that those closely connected with them receive appropriate support? In this chapter we seek to identify the basic theological problem which Alex poses for us. It will be argued that it is the problem of the worth and salvation of human beings generally. We shall also outline the theological criteria to be used in assessing solutions to that problem. Having established these preliminary points, we shall be in a position to investigate responses to the problem in the remaining chapters of this study.

The theological problem posed by people who are handicapped is sometimes considered to be a form of the problem of suffering. This problem arises for theists because their faith in God as a loving creator and caring providence appears to them to be irreconcilable with cases of suffering due to natural processes.

The problem is particularly pressing in those cases where the suffering cannot be justified on the grounds that it supports beneficial and punishes destructive behaviour. The pain from a scorched finger, for example, may be held to teach us to be careful with fire, while a hangover may be seen as a punishment for having drunk too freely! It is not possible, however, to imagine lessons and penalties which justify the sufferings of an infant whose limbs have

38

repeatedly to be punctured and restrained for drips, of a child struggling to breathe because of asthma, or of an old person confused because of senile dementia. To suggest that such states are warranted because they give opportunities for others to show their love and skill is demonic. However admirable the care shown by some, and however amazing some medical techniques, the world would be a happier environment for personal fulfilment if we did not need hospitals and if medical science was just as much a matter of purely intellectual delight as the study of quantum gravity seems to be.

The problem of suffering is classically presented in the form of a dilemma. Either God *cannot* or God *will not* put an end to pointless suffering in the world. If God *cannot* end it, then God is not all-powerful – and, it is assumed, a being that is not all-powerful is not authentically 'God'. If on the other hand God *will not* end suffering, then God is not wholly benevolent. A being that is not wholly benevolent, however, is similarly judged not to satisfy the defining characteristic of 'God'. As 'that than which a greater cannot be conceived' and 'the proper object of worship', God must be perfectly good in every respect.

There is no way of avoiding this dilemma by denying the reality of suffering. Experiences of its reality are too common for this to be a credible option. People scream and writhe and moan. Their agonies are no illusion.

Nor does a theory of *karma* provide a satisfactory escape from the dilemma. Attempts to justify what some people experience by suggesting that individuals in one life may suffer for (their?) behaviour in a previous, unrecollected life are unconvincing. Not only has such a theory to find rationally convincing support for the presupposed notion of reincarnation, it also has to warrant the morality of imposing penalties on individuals for deeds done by persons with whom they have no sense of identity or succession. Does, then, the dilemma indicate that it is not justifiable to believe in the reality of God?

When the problem of suffering is posed in this way, it is not easy – perhaps it is not rationally possible – to find a satisfying solution to it. Those who are disturbed by the problem do not doubt that belief in the reality of God has

certain practical implications. According to their understanding, as the ground of being God must determine the
fundamental character of reality; as all-powerful, all-wise
and benevolent, God must be able and willing to eradicate
suffering. The other component of the problem, as has been
noted, is equally clear. People suffer, in some cases
horrifyingly. Frequently their sufferings appear pointless.
What happens to individuals has no predictable relationship
to what they need or deserve. In practice, therefore, it appears
either that there is no God or (which amounts in practice to
the same thing) that the divine reality is not utterly
beneficial.

Suffering thus appears to pose a fundamental problem for
faith in God. In chapter seven we shall return to this problem.
What is important to recognize here is that the problem
posed by handicap is not itself a form of the problem of
suffering. Severely handicapped people are not, of course,
exempt from suffering. Some have accidents; some get cancer
and kidney failure and heart-attacks; some itch with
chickenpox and ache with flu; some experience frustration,
disappointment and pain. In this they are like all other
people.

In some cases their handicaps aggravate their suffering.
Those who are incapable of learning the dangers of fire,
pollution and traffic will not be aware of the need to protect
themselves from these dangers. An itch may annoy Robert; it
is all the more irritating for Mary whose paralysis prevents
her from rubbing the spot. Migraine is bad; to see but to be
unable to reach the tablets that give relief may well make it
feel worse. Those who are incapable of understanding what
is happening to them or of communicating what they feel
may find the experiences of pain and frustration all the more
disturbing. On the other hand, some handicaps may limit
suffering. People with restricted powers of anticipation, for
example, may have greater pleasure in their present
awareness of what is enjoyable because they have fewer
worries about the future. What is not imagined will not be
feared; what is not hoped for will not be missed.

Nevertheless, whatever the practical significance of these
differences between people, they do not show that people
with handicaps pose a theological problem which is peculiar

to them. So far as suffering is concerned, their position is basically the same as that of the supposedly non-handicapped. Some handicapped people are badly hurt on occasion; others suffer severe and prolonged pain. But so do some who are not regarded as handicapped. In many cases handicapped people apparently share the happy and unhappy 'run of the mill' experiences of life typical of human existence – with the variations found between individuals. Whatever, then, may be the problem highlighted by the condition of handicapped people, it is not to be identified as such with the problem of suffering, although, it should also be acknowledged, in many cases (where people lose their sight or are paralysed or are racked with pain, for example) that problem is also raised by the condition which renders people handicapped.

On the other hand, while the condition of handicapped people does not pose the problem of *suffering* in a special way, it may be considered to highlight the general problem of natural evil. A machine that failed on numerous occasions to do the job for which it was intended would be considered to have had an incompetent designer or a shoddy manufacturer. Seeing the effects of drought in the Sahara and of flood in Bangladesh, children with inherited AIDS and mature people destroyed by Huntington's chorea, it is tempting to agree with the farmer who, looking at a field of corn devastated by a storm, said, 'If I were God, I'd make a better job of organizing things.'

The farmer's remark is a blunt expression of the way in which those who believe in the reality of God normally understand the problem of natural evil. The presupposition of their understanding is that God as creator is responsible for the structures and processes of the natural world being as they are. In that case, they ask, is it justifiable to trust and worship God as supreme and perfect, both in creation and in providence, when what happens naturally prevents some individuals from enjoying the expectations of full human existence?

Any credible response to the problem of natural evil must begin by recognizing that the basis of living organisms is not secure. On a relatively minute number of occasions, for example, DNA and RNA macromolecules fail to replicate accurately or are altered by interactions with particles of radiation, whether of cosmic or of terrestrial origin. In most cases what results either has no significance or is self-destructive. In a very few cases a genetic abnormality or a cancerous mutation is produced. This may destroy the organism to which it belongs; on the other hand, though extremely rarely, it may be the source of an evolutionary development. On a far larger scale of being, the outworkings of physical processes are actualized in earthquakes, volcanoes, droughts and floods. While these may destroy some individual organisms, they may also bring about changes in the environment suitable for the development of other organisms.

Thus, in spite of the beauty, grandeur and wonderfully intricate processes (cf. the development of a child from a fertilized egg) observable in the natural world, things occur in it which seem to support Hume's suggestion that if the world has been divinely created, it makes sense to interpret it as either the work of an 'inferior Deity' whose effort is the object of 'derision to his superiors' or 'the product of old age and dotage in some superannuated Deity' (Hume 1935: 209)! The alternative is to consider what happens in specific cases as accidental. Not only atheistic scientists like Jacques Monod but also theistic ones like Arthur Peacocke maintain that the processes of nature are most appropriately understood as a product of chance and necessity. According to such an understanding God did not intend that a particular particle should collide with a particular molecule with a particular energy and direction to produce a particular result. Nor did God so organize affairs that that shower of rain occurred when the clothes on the line had dried. It just happened that way.

Since, however, God is commonly believed to have supreme power and wisdom, the reality of natural evils (i.e., of natural events which place obstacles in the way of human flourishing) is widely considered to raise questions about God's creative activity. Could – and, if so, should – God not have created the world in a way that such accidents did not occur? This seems to be a genuine theological problem. And, furthermore, the state of many handicapped people seems to pose the problem in an inescapable way. Is God justified in so ordering the creation that it comes about that some people are born without limbs or with defective organs or with severe learning difficulties, and that others inherit a genetic time-bomb that eventually destroys them?

This too is an issue to which we will return in chapter seven. It will be suggested there that the supposed theological problem of natural evil, like that of suffering, is a bogus one. It rests on unsupportable presuppositions about God, and in particular about what is meant by God's creative activity and providential power. For many who believe in God this may be a surprising conclusion. The reasons for it, however, will have to wait until the last part of that later chapter (although nothing prevents an impatient reader from taking a sneak preview of it). What it is important to recognize here is that just as handicap itself is not to be regarded as a form of suffering, so it is not to be regarded as necessarily a natural evil.

To assert that handicap is not necessarily a natural evil may be criticized as a harsh remark expressing a wrong judgement. How, critics may ask, can it be justifiable to maintain that it is not necessarily a natural evil for a child to be born without a hand or with Down's Syndrome or with Hirschprung's Disease or blind or deaf? In reply to such criticisms two things need to be said. Furthermore, it is important to distinguish between them.

The first is that to hold that handicap as such is not *necessarily* a natural evil is not to say that all forms of it are to be regarded with equanimity. Some forms of handicap are deeply disturbing. In this respect genetic malformations are properly to be joined with cases of storm, famine and disease in raising questions about what is to be understood by the doctrine of God as a benevolent creator and providence. This is an issue which is to be discussed in chapter seven.

The second comment is fundamental for clarifying the theological problem which is properly highlighted by the states of severely handicapped people and whose identification is the subject of this chapter. As was noted in the previous chapter, to be so handicapped is not necessarily as such to be judged to be a natural evil unless the finitude and variety characteristic of all forms of existence other than God's own mode of being are to be so judged. Instead of giving thanks to God that they are not like handicapped people (cf. Luke 18.11–14), those who consider themselves to be non-handicapped need to recognize that the limitations of handicapped people do not make them essentially different. What their handicaps do is to draw attention to the finitude of all being – and in particular to the finitude of all human being. Different people have different limits but no human being is infinite. Consequently, to judge handicap as such to be a natural evil – and perhaps, therefore, evidence of the creator's incompetence or ill-will – is to fail to recognize the essential distinction between the divine and the human, the creator and the created,

What, then, is the problem for faith and for theological understanding which is highlighted by the state of severely handicapped people? If it be correct to hold that it is that of the finitude of all human being, why is such finitude considered to present a problem? God alone is perfect, unsurpassable by others and limited only by the consequences of the divine reality and will. To be finite is the natural state of what is created and non-divine. Why should this essential characteristic of human being (and of all other non-divine states) be regarded as problematic, even as evil?

Not all natural states present problems to us. William Paley's *Natural Theology*, a classic exposition of the argument from design, begins with this sentence:

> In crossing a heath, suppose I pitched my foot against a *stone*, and were asked how the stone came to be there: I might possibly answer, that, for anything I knew to the contrary, it had lain there for ever; nor would it perhaps be very easy to show the absurdity of this answer. (Paley 1837: 1)

In his day most people would have been satisfied with this answer. Underlying their satisfaction was the sense that on the whole natural states of affairs are not problematic. They are what happens to be the case and, as such, mark the end of questioning.

Today Paley's answer might not be as readily satisfying.

The extension of scientific modes of questioning in the past two centuries means that it is often not sufficient to point out on a superficial level that this is how things happen to be. In the case of the stone, for example, people with geological and geographical interests might find *that* kind of rock in *that* particular location puzzling. They might want to know how *that* had come to be *there*. The question will be answered when they discover some prior state of affairs (e.g., glacial movement) which explains how what they now observe has come to be so. That prior state may, in turn, also provoke questions about how it came to be. Nevertheless, at each stage the answer is the identification of a state of affairs. As Whitehead's 'ontological principle' puts it, 'actual entities are the only *reasons*; so that to search for a *reason* is to search for one or more actual entities' (Whitehead 1978: 24). Thus, while Paley's answer to a question about the presence of a stone might not satisfy everyone today, the principle behind his answer, namely, to identify at an appropriate level of explanation what happens to be the case, is the way by which the quest for understanding is satisfied.

Questioning stops when a state of affairs is identified of which all that can or needs to be said is, 'Well, that is how it is.' There is no natural fact which can provide an answer to the question, 'Why is the speed of light 186,000 miles per second?' That is what the speed of light happens to be. There is nothing more that can be explained. If, on the other hand, we notice a stone on a hillside, we may expect to find an answer to the question 'Why is it there?', but we are only likely to ask the question if it is unusual to find such a stone in such a habitat, or if we are investigating the geology of that hillside. In most cases we just walk past it. It is taken to be natural for it to be there; and because it is taken to be natural, it poses no problem for us.

Similarly there are many facts about the constitution of human being which are not considered to present problems for us. We accept them as being what is the case with us. In order to live we need to breathe oxygen: in an oxygen-free environment (such as on the surface of the moon), we can only survive with artificial support. We need to have vitamin C in our diet but we die if we swallow cyanide. We can naturally see objects only in terms of lightwaves whose length lies between those of red and violet light. We bleed if our skin is broken. People lived and did things before we were born, and there will be events that happen after we are dead. We can only be in one place at one time. Without mechanical means we cannot jump three metres above the earth's surface nor stay aloft.

People who complained that they are handicapped because they cannot do without oxygen and vitamin C, or because they cannot 'see' infra-red emissions, or because they could not have listened to both Cicero and Wesley would be regarded as very odd. Their complaint would generally be taken to indicate immaturity: they are failing to accept what has to be accepted because that is how things happen to be. And it is not easy to see how these states, apart perhaps from that of mortality, can be held to raise a theological problem, unless it is a problem that human reality is not as extensive and perfect as God's reality.

Furthermore, no theological problem is generally perceived to arise from the fact that some beings have qualities which are superior to those enjoyed by human beings. Horses can run faster than human beings. Dogs can hear 'sounds' at frequencies inaudible to human beings, and bats can locate echoes with precision impossible for human beings. Eagles have keener eyesight, elephants live longer, beavers have stronger teeth, hamsters breed faster and hippopotamuses can stay submerged longer than human beings. Newborn lambs are mobile far more quickly than human infants. All these comparisons are well known and do not evoke existential anxiety – at any rate not in normal human beings. They express the limits of human being when compared to that of other kinds of animal.

Nor, in spite of the Frankenstein nightmares of science fiction, does any theological problem emerge from the bare recognition that machines can calculate faster, mill more accurately, work more efficiently and are adaptable to more hostile environments than any human being. All that the comparisons indicate are the limitations of human being. The theological questions that do arise in this respect are not about humankind as such. They are about the ways in which people use machines and about the need to ensure that processes are not developed which could harm humankind or even make this planet uninhabitable.

Comparisons can also be made between individuals. John Ray saw the wisdom of God manifested among other things in 'the Variety of Lineaments in the Faces of Men', for, as he pointed out, if we all looked exactly alike, we would not be able to distinguish the person who robbed us or the person who had agreed a contract with us from everyone else (Ray 1722: 245)! While Ray's positive appraisal of differences between individuals belongs to a version of the argument from design that no longer convinces, neither are the differences between human beings normally perceived to present a theological problem. The person who stands behind me in a crowd may be irritated by my height, and a friend may pity me because I prefer the loneliness of a mountain to the conviviality of a pub, but these are characteristics that help to identify me as me – as are my baldness and the colour of my eyes. Persons differ.

Nor is a serious theological problem usually considered to arise from the way in which people generally differ in their abilities. The person next to me in worship may be put off by my inability to sing in tune but that is just another of the characteristics that mark me out as me. More serious are the frustrations that some people feel in not being able to do what others do and what they want to do. As I teach my students I am aware that some find it easy to grasp and argue about the forms of the ontological argument presented by Anselm, Descartes and Leibniz and developed by Hartshorne while others find the elusive abstractions hard (and in some cases apparently impossible) to master. The difficulties of the latter not only pose problems for me as a teacher: How can I explain the issues in a way that they can grasp them? They also make me feel sorry for them as they struggle to understand an argument but cannot manage it. In some cases what individuals want to do differs considerably from what they can achieve – as examination results illustrate. Nevertheless, the different degrees of intellectual competence revealed by my students is not a theological problem as such. It is another expression of how things are. People differ – in some cases very considerably – in intellectual capability, physical prowess, aesthetic awareness and emotional responsiveness.

Some people, however, have perceived a moral problem in these differences. They consider it unfair that people differ: all should be alike, at least in having the same potentialities. No one ought to have the privilege of capabilities which others do not share. Whereas initially this may seem a just judgement, even if one that puts forward an ideal state which is in sharp contrast to the actual state of human being, further reflection suggests that this ideal state may not be as attractive as at first appears. For one thing, if this were the case, any failure on my part to use the skills that others employ in completing a task would be liable to be deemed to be my own fault. I must have had the latent ability: that I did not perform the task as well as others was because I had not developed the talents available to me. This would be a burden which would not be easy to bear. Secondly, behind this supposed ideal lies a bureaucratic uniformism which apparently presupposes that humankind would be perfect if all its members were as alike as the red balls on a snooker table. It is not an appealing prospect. In any case, if for no other reason than that the genetic construction of human beings ensures variety (providing that cloning never becomes a real possibility for humankind), it will never come about. Where attempts have been made to enforce such a uniform society, the costs have been appalling. The massacres by the Pol Pot regime were not an accident. They were due to a ruthless and deliberate attempt to produce a uniformitarian society – and the privileges grasped by party officials remind us that those who seek to establish uniformity are always under severe temptation to exempt themselves, and more frequently than not succumb to the temptation!

Although the fact of differences between people does not raise a theological problem, it does raise a moral issue, namely, that of the obligation on people to develop their own capabilities and of the obligation on society to seek to eradicate as far as possible obstacles which prevent this. Furthermore, where questions of moral evaluation arise, there is also the need to remember that in certain respects (perhaps the most important respects morally) people should be judged by how far they have realized their potentials rather than by their successes in satisfying some attainment targets. This is the moral of the story of the widow's coins (cf. Luke 21.1ff). It may appear trite but it is often forgotten in the competitive structures of society. Much as my students may doubt it, I do not think it is important that they master the ontological argument, process thought and the anthropological conditioning of theological judgements! What is important is that they use their opportunities to develop their own understanding to the full.

In spite of the above considerations, there are nevertheless some who still allege that differences between people constitute a form of the problem of evil. They fasten on the fact that some people are frustrated because, no matter how hard they try, they cannot equal the attainments of others in some respect or other. From this it is inferred that the state of humankind (as of the animal realm – cf. the battles between bucks: only one can win the does) leads to disappointment for some. On these grounds it is held not to be a fit product of a fair and benevolent creator. This judgement presupposes a view of the divine creativity which will be questioned in chapter seven.

In some cases the feeling of disappointment and frustration is justified. There is nothing to be criticized in a mother when she feels frustrated because poverty or famine prevents her feeding her children, or in a surgeon when she feels disappointed because arthritis in her hands has stopped her using her skills to relieve suffering. It is similarly not only understandable but also unexceptionable for handicapped people to feel disappointed and frustrated when they find themselves lacking basic powers which people normally have, and, in particular, powers which are essential for existence as an autonomous self. On the other hand, it also needs to be noted that, unlike what is assumed by some educational and political pundits, it is not clear that every case of disappointment and frustration is necessarily wrong – especially if the source of disappointment and frustration is a desire for what is not realistically available to the person. We smile at the baby who cries for the moon. It is not available. Political movements similarly have to temper their visions for society with what is in practice possible, given the resources of this world, if they are not to be ridiculed as utopian dreams. If human beings were never to be disappointed, they would presumably have to be God. Instead, therefore, of regarding every form of disappointment and frustration as posing a form of the problem of evil, it is more enlightening theologically to perceive that in some cases their ultimate source may be a failure to recognize that we are not God – and that that failure is the source of sin.

Those who find in differences between individuals a form of the problem of evil generally imply that there is, or at least that there should be, a standard blueprint of the human, and hence that ideally we should all be identical – a series of individuals as indistinguishable from each other as red snooker balls. As has been suggested, this is a bureaucratic vision of uniformity gone mad. While it must not be forgotten that some forms of handicap constrict and even destroy personal life, it must also be remembered that the aesthetic richness of life requires variety in it. It is wrong, furthermore, to accept uncritically the values and attainments of our own culture as the basis for judging others. Modern anthropological studies have shown that this is a blinkered way of understanding. It may blind us to riches in other cultures and forms of society.

Theologically the uniformitarian approach leads to attempts to grasp the divine will in terms of what a priori we envisage to be the best. A more appropriate theological approach takes seriously what in fact we discover to be the case in reality – on the grounds that what actually is so may throw some light on the nature of the divine will. When this principle is followed, the conclusion seems to have to be that the divine will does not seek uniformity. If the opposite were the case, the cosmos would presumably be something like a series of perfect, identical spheres. This is a view which theologians in the past, under the influence of Greek thought about perfection, tried to impose upon the creator and the created. What actually is the case in the cosmos is not like that. Reflection indicates, furthermore, that such a cosmos would be utterly dull. Beauty is found in the experience of the tension between harmony and contrast. Therefore it is not surprising to find that examination of what actually occurs in the cosmos indicates that the creativity of the divine is to be conceived in terms of the exploration and enjoyment of variety. Is it a parable of the divine creativity that while to the careless a snowfield looks uniform, those who take care to examine the individual flakes constituting it claim that no two are identical?

Does the position change when we take into account those who are handicapped, especially those who are severely handicapped? It is easy to maintain that the divine will is for variety when we are comparing the different gifts of mathematical students and theological students, or of rugby players and poets. Like snowflakes, each form may be appreciated as having worth in an individual way. It is not difficult to maintain it when we counsel someone who has not passed (or not passed as well as he or she had hoped) an examination, or has not succeeded in getting on the team, or has been thwarted in love. People differ, we can point out, and 'the important thing is that you are you, not that you succeed in doing what someone else can do'.

This is largely uncontroversial so long as we are dealing with most people. Indeed, if we find their sense of self-worth destroyed because they have not achieved some particular goal, we may well (and justifiably) become irritated with them as well as sad for them. Why do they think that they are so hard done by in not gaining that prize, even if they had set their hearts on it? Some people, however, judge that a radically different situation arises when we consider the state of handicapped people, especially of those who are severely handicapped. Why is this?

They perceive a problem where they consider that a handicapped person's condition prevents her or him from enjoying the full life which they believe to be God's will for everyone. In such a case the handicapped person's limitations, be they physical, mental, emotional or aesthetic, are considered by them to prevent that person having the capacity for fulfilling the proper expectations for human existence. Furthermore, as was noted in the previous chapter, whereas feminist, black and political forms of liberation theology press the need for 'liberation' from external oppressors, theological understanding of such a handicapped person is concerned with limitations which are apparently intrinsic to his or her being and which, at present at any rate, are predominantly unchangeable. The nub of the problem, then, is that the characteristics of at least some severely handicapped persons are considered to make it impossible for those people to have the potential for sharing in the quality of life that is regarded as typically human. As a result some severely handicapped people are not only considered to be incapable of enjoying human existence to the full; they may even be regarded by some people as being not fully human, although it may be regarded as impolite to state this explicitly.

This view may be criticized on three counts.

Firstly, a person who deems those who do not share his or her characteristics as less than fully human may be criticized for presuming to adopt the role of God. According to a traditional understanding of the doctrine of divine creativity, the specifications for each type of creature are decided by God. What is and what is not human, therefore, is accordingly to be determined by reference to those specifications. So far as I know, however, no such specifications are available for inspection at God's patent office. In any case, the presupposed understanding of creation as God's implementation of divine designs seems irreconcilable (in spite of the desperate attempts of some creationists) with what now appear to be well-established findings about the evolution of species. Suggestions about a blueprint which specifies the distinctive characteristics of human being – or the being of any other type of creature – are the result of imposing human imaginations upon the concept of the divine rather than a recognition of what actually happens. Species evolve by chance alterations in genetic templates, not by the deliberate production of prototypes or by the planned modification of previous productions.

The doctrine that the human is distinctive in being in 'the image of God' (which will be discussed further in chapter seven) offers no material guidance towards determining what is and what is not authentically human being. Although frequently affirmed, the doctrine does not make clear what are the defining material boundaries of being in that 'image'. Instead it merely asserts that *whatever* – or, perhaps, better *whoever* – is human has a relationship to the divine which is not shared by other creatures. While theologians identify the nature of that relationship in various ways (seeing it, for example, as referring to the rational, or the moral, or the creative, or the autonomous, or the playful, or the worshipping, or the familial character of human being), their identifications seem to be products of their analyses of human being and their notions of the divine rather than an application to the human of what is independently known about God's will.

Consequently attempts to define the limits of authentic human being by reference to a divine specification of that being are to be rejected. No such specification is available. Those who claim to know the content of one and to be able thereby to identify those who are not properly human are in practice applying distinctions which arise from human understanding. Hence they are acting as if they are God. Such presumption is unwarrantable.

Secondly, attempts to distinguish between those who have and those who do not have the capacity for full human being on the grounds of ability to fulfil a particular material norm assume that there is such a norm by which human beings should be judged. It may be held, for example, that to be fully human entails the ability to live autonomously, or to reason, or to be imaginatively creative, or to be self-aware of oneself as a person in relationship with other persons. The variety of ways in which the norm may be identified indicates that this assumption is debatable in practice. It is clearly open to anyone who disputes the validity of discriminating by one norm (or set of norms) to deny that that is the appropriate norm for human being and to offer a different one.

Debates about *which* norm is correct for distinguishing human being may, however, beg the question. There may not be such a norm or set of norms. It is arguable that whereas bureaucratic agencies can lay down standards for determining what is to be regarded as a saleable apple, a screw or a dairy cow, properly human being is not to be distinguished from the less than fully human or from the non-human by the satisfaction of a certain standard. What it is to be human is what human beings make of their being. This is the underlying truth in the claim of existentialist thinkers that for human beings 'existence precedes essence'.

An individual's thoughts and actions determine what it is to be human in the case of that person.

What this implies theologically is that the divine is not to be thought of as having either an overall goal for all persons to fulfil in some appropriate way or a particular goal for each individual – the notion of a specific 'vocation' to which he or she is 'called' individually by God. Instead of such traditional doctrines, God's will is rather to be considered as a will that each individual be that individual. The divine does not value individuals according to the extent to which they satisfy norms or goals external to themselves. God appreciates to the full the values that are realized in an individual being by that individual becoming what he or she comes to be.

God shared what Alex experienced, enjoying what he enjoyed, suffering what he suffered and being worried by what worried him. Alex, in other words, was embraced, cherished and valued by God as who Alex was each moment. Each moment of his being, furthermore, is everlastingly preserved in the awareness of Alex in the divine memory. And the same is the case with each human being. God is greater than the rule-imposing image of supremacy by which theists have frequently fashioned God. As the loving creator who, unlike human rulers, is not troubled by inferiority complexes, God has the confidence to allow people to be themselves and to accept them for what they actually are. God cares for every person – in their pettiness and nastiness (which God wills to be transformed) as well as in their love and creativity (which God desires to be enhanced). For God there is no point on a scale which persons must surpass in order to be accepted or to be regarded as properly human.

Thirdly, people who deem inferior, even less than fully human, those who do not share their characteristics may be criticized for entertaining a 'master-race' delusion. This delusion happens when one group of people regards certain characteristic qualities (almost always their own), whether racially or culturally moulded, as the norm for what it is to be properly human. This delusion needs to be recognized for what it is and rejected. It is fundamentally wrong. This is not simply because of the practical implications of entertaining such a position – although they would be appalling if they were considered (as has been and still is the case in some places) to warrant the oppression of those deemed to fail to meet the norm and hence to be regarded as less than fully human. No group of people, however large or however dominant, can justifiably claim a Procrustean right to provide the defining characteristics of authentic human being. The reason for this is that what defines the boundary of human being is not race or culture or skill or potential but basic genetic belonging. What it is to be human is whatever individuals who genetically belong to the species become, whether by unconscious acculturation or by deliberate choice – or, as generally happens, as a messy mixture of both – within the limits of each individual's potential.

This biological way of defining the limits of authentic humanity may initially seem surprising. It is, of course, a somewhat circular definition since people are classed as human because their parents are so classed, and they in turn are so classed because their parents are so classed . . . In view of the evolutionary development of human being, the line back will eventually lead to beings whose status is puzzling. Were they human beings or not? For the purposes of the discussion here, however, that aspect of the question of classification can be ignored. With the possible exception of cases like that of the (mythical?) yeti, there is no dispute today about which living beings are to be classed biologically as human beings, however varied their lifestyles and values, and which are not.

Nor for our purposes here is it necessary to reach decisions in the highly controversial disputes about, on the one hand, the point at which a human being starts to be such rather than, say, a foetus or an embryo or a bundle of fertilized cells; or, on the other hand, the point at which human being ceases to be such and is to be regarded as an artificially sustained organism with no potential for self-consciousness, let alone for the thought and activity of independent being. Whether abortion, for example, is to be judged as murder (because it is to be regarded as killing a human being) or as the morally legitimate removal of a group of cells (because it is the excision from a body of what is regarded as not yet human), the living offspring which has developed from an egg of a human mother fertilized by a sperm from a human father is to be recognized from birth to be a human being. It is only in science fiction that problems of identification arise because of the combination of a human and a non-human parent.

While, then, in the past some settlers may have felt no compunction about killing native inhabitants because they did not consider them as human beings, such attitudes are no longer acceptable, even if they ever seemed to be so, to morally aware persons. It is impossible to envisage that a court of law, having determined that A killed B, and having identified both B and B's parentage, would find any difficulty in deciding that A's act was murder because it is not clear whether B was or was not a human being. Whatever plausible defences may be open to killers, doubt about whether their victims were human beings, once their identity and parentage are known, is not one of them. The human status of the victims is clear.

Would it, however, be advisable to try to produce a satisfactory non-biological definition of the authentically human to augment, if not to replace, the genetic one? And, if so, would it be possible to justify one? Reflection on these questions suggests that it would be neither advisable nor possible. It would not be advisable because the adoption of any such set of characteristics – based, for instance, on the possession of physical skills or practical abilities or mental capacity or cultural inheritance – would most likely not only select and endorse the typical characteristics of those promoting the set but, more disturbingly, would then seem to permit the promoters to treat as not fully human those who did not share those characteristics. The cases of genocide and oppression that have resulted from the adoption of such a 'master-race' view of human being warn against it. It is, in any case, not possible to find a justifiable non-biological basis for identifying human being because of the variety of what is generally acceptable as such being. This variety indicates that any set of characteristics which were selected would be open to the fundamental challenge that it begged the question. Why should this set rather than that set be definitive of human being?

When the case of severely handicapped persons like Alex is considered in the light of the above considerations, it becomes clear that being handicapped as such does not present a genuine *theological* problem. In the initial outline of this study I wrote that the 'identification of handicap as a problem can be criticized on the grounds that those who see it as such are using their collective self-understanding as a norm for determining what is God's will for human being. They are thus liable to fall into one or both of two traps. The first trap is that of (unconsciously) assuming that they are God – in the sense that their self-understanding of human being is the standard for all persons. The second is that of believing that they know the will of God for human being in general, and for this human being in particular.' This I still hold, as the above discussion indicates.

In the draft, however, I went on to say that 'on the other hand it would be a mistake to consider that handicap does not present a problem for theistic faith. In Alex's case, his enjoyment of life was limited and his potential for self-expression and autonomous living was severely restricted. *If* to be human is to be in the image of God, *if* this is the will of God for every person, and *if* the notion of being "in the image of God" refers at least in part to the possibility of a significant degree of creative and autonomous living (and the last "if" is particularly controversial and, as will be indicated in chapter seven, is one that I reject), then the condition of severely handicapped people poses a problem for theistic faith in that the conditions which identify them as handicapped indicate that they seem to have markedly restricted potential in these respects.' Alex's mother objected to this. She maintained that such comments express 'our arrogance and presumption'.

To the extent that these comments in any way disparage Alex's worth, she was right. As we shall consider in the next chapter, anyone who is handicapped, however severely, has as much – and as little – worth as any other person. Furthermore, while in many (if not in all) cases their handicaps restrict the range of enjoyments open to handicapped people, being so confined does not mean that handicapped people are unable to share the intensity of experience and depth of delight enjoyed by others. Indeed, their limitations may help them to an intensity and depth that others are too easily distracted from achieving. In these respects, then, those who are severely handicapped may seem to pose a problem for others only because those others unwarrantably consider that their own state is the norm for judging the worth of a human being. Alex's mother perceived more quickly than I did the need to revise my initial remarks.

Nevertheless, while no handicap, however great, diminishes the worth of a person, some handicaps do seriously limit at least the ranges of enjoyment open to those who suffer from them. A keen swimmer who has a withered limb has to recognize that no amount of effort will bring him or her the excitement of taking part in open competitions on equal terms; a blind person will never know the delight of a view from a summit or have the freedom taken for granted by sighted people in climbing mountains or in hurrying for a seat on a crowded train. Handicapped people who are aware that there are experiences which they either miss entirely or can enjoy only in circumscribed ways may accordingly ask why they suffer in this way. Their question is not to be ignored.

As severely handicapped people compare themselves with others, they may well feel deprived. Life may be felt to have cheated them. They find no comfort in being told that everyone is finite and that they just happen to be more limited than others. They may justifiably judge that answer to be as unsatisfying as the multi-millionaire's comment to the single-parent with a sick child having to survive off social security payments, 'We all have to live within our means: I too cannot buy everything I would like.' All may be finite, but different limits of finitude result in importantly different possibilities. In principle, however, the question which they ask is not peculiar to handicapped people. It is one expression of the general problem of suffering to be considered in chapter seven. Whether, therefore, the limitations which identify handicapped people as such are considered by others or by the handicapped themselves, they do not appear to pose a special theological problem.

Nevertheless, when we consider the condition of handicapped people, a theological problem does arise. What is it?

The theological problem posed by handicapped people is that of the worth of human being as such. Initially the question posed by them may seem to be the double one: What is the worth of the lives of those whose capacities are severely limited, and what may credibly be held to be the meaning of the 'gospel', the 'good news' of salvation, for them? Reflection reveals, however, that the particularity of this question is unjustified. Handicapped people do not raise the basic issue in a unique way. What they do – and what other people may find uncomfortable – is to draw attention to the limitations of *all* human being and thereby to press home the question of the fundamental worth of each human being.

Those who are described as severely handicapped are not distinct in being limited in their understanding, restricted in their abilities, and finite in their being. While the differences between individuals are important in certain respects, every person is to some extent limited, restricted and finite. This is what it is to be human rather than divine. Since this is so, the theological question that properly arises is not: What is the worth of and salvation for handicapped people? The question that must be faced is: What is the worth of and salvation for human beings – that is, for each and every person?

The reason why many people find themselves uncomfortable in the company of a handicapped stranger may not be because they are uncertain about how to converse with her or him. Nor may it simply be because they are uncertain how to avoid upsetting him or her by making tactless remarks. A deeper, although generally unacknowledged, reason may be that the state of the handicapped person threatens their sense of security. While that state may in one respect make them feel thankful that they are not so afflicted, it may also remind them that their own well-being is contingent. Not only the opportunities provided by their socio-economic and cultural situation but also their genetic inheritance and natural capabilities are a matter of luck. Furthermore, whatever capacities they presently enjoy may be taken away by disease, accident and ageing.

The following incident illustrates the point. Two young men helped an elderly lady into a restaurant. She was very deaf and unable to walk unaided. She did not seem greatly aware of her surroundings. When she sat down she chain-smoked and her ash fell on and around her rather than in the ashtray. Her friends brought her two glasses of sherry and a large ice-cream sundae. She enjoyed them, scooping up some of the cream, ice and fruit from the table-cloth where her trembling hand had dropped it. When she left, a man at a nearby table remarked, 'I wish they would not bring people like that in here. It spoils the atmosphere.' Why could he not enjoy that old lady's delight at her sherry and sundae? What was the 'atmosphere' that was supposedly spoiled? I do not know – I was not brave enough to upset him further by asking – but I wondered if it was his illusion that he was the master of his fate, that he was in control of his life, that he had power and freedom to choose what he would do. The elderly lady had made him aware, although probably more unconsciously than consciously, that whatever autonomy a person may have in the prime of life, it is likely not to persist to the end – and that eventually there will be an end. Human beings are mortal.

We need to recognize, furthermore, that we are not merely restricted by things that happen to us through disease, accident and ageing as well by our socio-economic and cultural context. We are all limited throughout our lives. While comparisons may highlight the ways in which some persons surpass others in certain respects – for instance, in the ability to understand mathematics or to throw a ball or to sing in tune – we must not overlook the contingent and limited character of each human life and of human being itself. Human self-understanding begins with the recognition of its basic finitude.

To return, then, to the starting-point: the question posed by Alex is not the arrogant question: What was the worth of his life and what was the 'gospel' for him?, as posed by those who assume that his life was fundamentally different in kind from that of people who are generally considered not to be handicapped. The fundamental question posed by Alex is: What is the worth of any human life and what does the 'gospel' offer to each person? What Alex and others like him do is to bring home to us that no convincing answer to that question is to be found by ignoring our finitude and arrogating to ourselves, albeit implicitly, the qualities of the divine. Clear self-awareness, as Schleiermacher emphasizes, perceives that everyone is ultimately dependent (cf. Schleiermacher 1928:16).

As we consider our situation, we tend to absolutize our

standpoint. Looking out on 'our' world and trying to make sense of it, we are drawn towards a Ptolemaic attitude. Although we may admit that it is wrong to think of the creator as arranging the stars and planets for our benefit, our vanity makes it difficult for us to come to terms with the implications of Copernican and Darwinian thought about nature, and of Enlightenment and psychoanalytic thought about history and individual existence. Credible human self-understanding needs to take account of the cosmic, the biological, the historical and the personal aspects of human finitude.

Cosmically human being has existed for only a minute fraction of the history of a planet which orbits an ordinary star situated at an unremarkable position in a spiral arm of one of the huge number of galaxies that constitute the known cosmos. The emergence of that planet was a matter of cosmic chance. Its predicted dissolution into its dying sun will have no cosmic interest. This kind of event will have happened many times before and will be repeated many times afterwards.

Biologically, human being has emerged on this planet through a hit-and-miss evolutionary process of accidental mutations in DNA chains with vastly more unproductive than fruitful developments. It has not existed for very long and will eventually become extinct, whether like the dinosaur because of natural processes or like the dodo because of human activity. It is unjustified (and Ptolemaic) hubris to consider, as some forms of the anthropic principle suggest, that the enormous remoteness of the chance emergence of human being within the cosmos indicates that there is some underlying necessity about it. Things just happen to have occurred that way.

The historical existence of human beings in civilized societies is much briefer than its biological existence. Whatever our proper pride in humankind's achievements, the evidence of the past is predominantly a record of perishing. States, empires and even civilizations have collapsed. Ruins in the jungle, triumphal columns in museums, robbed burial chambers and obsolete steam-engines are monuments to glory that has departed. What were the latest ideas and state-of-the-art technologies of our forefathers often seem amusingly dated to us. Why should we expect today's culture and artefacts to survive?

Individual existence is even more ephemeral. We do not know the names, let alone the personal characters, of the great ones who were buried in the Long Barrows. And who were the workers who raised those mounds? Apart from the odd scratch on a slab or a broken tool, there is no trace of those individuals. No one now knows the persons who chipped stone tools at Penmaenmawr or erected Zimbabwe. Genetic research has been claimed to show (although the conclusion is disputed) that all the native inhabitants of America are descended from four women. Who were they? What did they hope and fear, want and cherish? We cannot know. Even where names have survived on old gravestones, the personalities which they identify have merged into the indistinguishing soil of the past.

When, therefore, we appreciate the character of human being, it is not only in the case of those like Alex that questions arise about worth and salvation. The cosmic, biological, historical and individual nature of such being renders the differences between persons unimportant. All are finite: temporary products of chance whose own products perish, they have no intrinsic significance. We are thus brought to ask with the author of Psalm 8 (although the answer developed in this study will be different from his somewhat arrogant one) what is the worth and destiny of humankind. The question is particular as well as general. What is the worth of this and that individual human being – of Alex and you and me – as well as of the human race as a whole?

This, then, is the question that my encounter with Alex and reflection on that encounter has provoked for me. It will be argued in the following chapters that the only satisfactory positive answer to that question is that, in spite of the chancy nature of human existence, God bestows worth upon each human being by appreciating her or him as an individual, even if that person is always extremely restricted in his or her awareness of and response to the world around. Therefore, while credible theistic understanding must recognize on the one hand that God as ultimate is the ground of all being, value and rationality, on the other it must assert that not only human being in general but also each human being in particular has significance for God and so has ultimate worth because of God. As Kierkegaard observed, this latter claim seems absurd. It is far more ridiculous than holding that 'the mightiest emperor that ever lived' was concerned about a poor day-labourer. It maintains that 'every individual, whatever in other respects this individual may be, man, woman, serving-maid, minister of state, merchant, barber, student, etc., – this individual exists *before* God' and 'is invited to live on the most intimate terms with God!' (Kierkegaard 1955: 216). Like every other person, then, Alex has ultimate worth because, and only because, God values him.

On what basis, however, is any answer to the question of the worth of human being to be judged? Although I am a philosophical theologian who enjoys wrestling with abstract and abstruse technicalities of the subject, I do not intend to become involved in such discussions here. On the other hand, in what follows I want to consider what Christian faith in God may be understood to affirm in response to the problem posed for me by Alex in a way that satisfies the proper criteria of theological understanding. There are four such criteria: appropriateness, credibility, adequacy, and practice.

Appropriateness is a matter of loyalty to the resources which are to be used in arriving at faith's self-understanding. For Christians these resources are in part provided by what they recognize as normative sources for and definitive statements of the contents of their faith. Formally these expressions are usually identified with the scriptures, doctrinal formulae and liturgies authorized by the Christian community and with the expositions of their contents in the writings of generally recognized teachers. The Christian faith, however, is not simply a matter of elucidating the contents of certain foundational propositions. It is an attempt to discern the ultimate nature of what is and what is to be. Accordingly, another part of its basic resources is provided by the data of common human experience and the consequent perception of the processes of reality. Its self-understanding is thus a product of the mutual interaction of the resources of faith's claims and the informations of experience.

This means that in practice the resources which mould Christian understanding of the nature and will of God in relation to human being are not precisely codified dogmatic propositions. They are constituted by the ways in which formally recognized materials are used within the believing community as they interact with what is found to be the case in reality. As a result the test of appropriateness is a matter of referring to a somewhat amorphous and developing tradition of faith and practice. When, therefore, a theological claim is made, the criterion of appropriateness is not satisfied by finding a 'proof text' in the officially recognized materials that apparently endorses it. Rather it is satisfied by showing how that claim is to be regarded as an authentic component of the ongoing – and elusive – cumulative tradition of Christian understanding.

Credibility, the second criterion, refers to the test of rational justifiability. Christian self-understanding is not a matter of formulating an attractive story about a never-never-land – a kind of comforting fairy story to lull believers to sleep. It is an attempt to determine what is the case. Since, furthermore, God is the ultimate reality, nothing that is truly perceived can be alien to the divine. Although, then, the results may be uncomfortable, Christian faith in God demands that its self-understanding be finally determined not by its inherited cumulative tradition but by what may warrantably be held to be true (whatever qualifications self-critical reason shows to be necessary to recognize the relativity of any claim to perceive the truth). Those who regard faith in God as the rejection of critical reason in favour of the entertainment of traditional doctrines may not be merely credulous. Their stance amounts to atheism if they prefer received traditions, however sacrosanct they may be claimed to be, to the demands of truth.

The third criterion is that of adequacy. This criterion requires that theological understanding offers insights that are recognized to be fundamentally significant not only by theologians but also by ordinary people. Since faith is a matter of actual living in the real world, its important insights are not high abstractions which intrigue those addicted to brain-teasers. They are insights which make sense of what people today recognize to be the character of their existence as human beings. I sometimes call this criterion 'the Bright Hour Test'. While the elderly ladies who attend the 'Bright Hour' in the local church may not be widely read in the latest philosophical and theological debates (they have more important things to see to, like making their pension last out and looking after a sick neighbour), they have rich and varied experiences of life. The challenge to theological understanding is to show that what it affirms makes sense of those experiences in ways that they can appreciate to be significant.

The final criterion is that of practice. Theistic faith is not just a matter of entertaining ideas, however true and adequate. It involves trust in God that is actualized in life. Thus of any claim to theological self-understanding, it is proper to ask: Does it work?

The preliminary discussions are now over. It is time to turn to substantive issues. Bearing in mind the above criteria, what is to be affirmed about the worth and salvation of human beings when we consider the insights into the nature of human being given by Alex?

4

Handicaps are not the will of God

As was suggested in the previous chapter, the least unsatisfactory way of defining the class of human beings is probably the genetic – and circular – one that anyone who is the living offspring of human beings is a human being. Nevertheless, while no other quality may safely be held to be necessary for human being, certain characteristics are so widely found in human beings that they may be considered typical features. Among them are the capacities to play, to celebrate, to imagine, to worship, and to create. Another feature is indicated by the species title, *homo sapiens*. Although much of the behaviour of human beings, both corporately and individually, may not seem to display much 'wisdom' (*sapientia*), it is typical of human beings to be inquisitive. Many of us – including, presumably, all who choose to read books like this – find ourselves subject to a basic drive to understand.

When, therefore, something happens which catches our attention, we try to make sense of it. We generally seek to achieve this by finding answers to two questions. The first is: 'What is it?' Here we seek concepts to classify what we have noticed. Identification, however, is not enough to satisfy understanding. As Kant suggests in the *Critique of Pure Reason*, one of the fundamental categories which structure our understanding is that of cause and effect. Accordingly, once we have identified what has occurred, we then ask: 'What caused it to happen?' Here we look for factors which brought it about – a nail which punctured the tyre, water in the plug which caused a short-circuit and made the circuit-breaker trip, infected meat that made the lecturer ill and led to the cancellation of her class, mutual antipathies which rendered the consultation unproductive. Although the relevant chain of causal connections may be long and complex, we are not intellectually satisfied until we have discerned the linked factors which resulted in the event.

Often the quest for understanding is satisfied when it has identified the relevant causal nexus. Because *this* was the case (a nail on the road, a leaking vase . . .), *that* happened (a puncture, a tripped circuit-breaker . . .). There seems to be nothing more to discover: what happened makes sense to us. No longer is it a problem. We understand it.

Sometimes, however, we are not so satisfied. We go on to ask of the initial event in the causal sequence or of the sequence itself, 'But why did it happen?' Here we are looking for a reason, a purpose or an intention (or a collection of them), which gives point to the event even if it does not justify it. Nails do not come to be on roads of their own accord. Why, then, was the nail on the road? If someone put it there deliberately, why did that person do this? If someone dropped it by accident, was that person being culpably careless?

Where human actions are involved, we are generally clear about the kind of factors that are appropriate for answering the question 'Why?' An answer of the order, 'She put nails on the road because she did not want him to leave' or, 'He had not noticed that the bag containing the nails had a rent in it' gives the kind of reason that is sought. They make sense of the cause of the event (a punctured tyre) because they give a reason for it. The quest for understanding is then satisfied.

Actions of which we may properly ask the question 'Why?' may not be limited to those of human beings. Although the appropriate answers may be less certain (because we have to use analogies derived from our awareness of our own behaviour), it may well be considered justifiable to ask, 'Why did the horse bolt?' and to answer the question by giving such a reason as, 'Because it was frightened by a helicopter.' Differences in modes of awareness (and even more of self-awareness) presumably mean that fear in the case of a horse is not exactly the same as fear experienced by a human being. Nevertheless, the behaviour of the horse is widely regarded as sufficiently comparable to that of a frightened human being for this answer to the question about the 'reason' for what happened to make sense. In contrast, the legitimacy of attempts to explain the behaviour of a sunflower in turning to face the sun by reference to intentions (and hence presupposing, even by extended analogy, notions of consciousness and will) is much more questionable. As for the case of the alignment of a compass needle, the question, 'Why does it do it?', when that question looks for an answer in terms of reasons, intentions and purposes, is mistaken in principle. In spite of the attempts of panpsychists, psychicalists and neo-animists to affirm the contrary, notions of reasons, intentions and purposes, however attenuated, seem not to make sense in the case of a compass needle, whether we consider the object as a whole or the individuals (whether at the level of crystals, molecules, atoms or particles) which constitute it.

In many situations we accept this. When a father smacks a stone over which his young daughter has tripped and says, 'Naughty stone!', we know that really there is no blame to be attached to the stone. The father's action may help to pacify his crying daughter by giving her an illusion of justified revenge but we know that the stone did not act intentionally. It just happened to be in his daughter's way. Similarly, when his daughter cannot have a picnic because it is raining, it is regrettable but there is no personal agency that is blameable. As we say, giving cold comfort, 'It is just one of those things that happen!'

So long as an event is not very important, the inappropriateness of asking, 'What is the reason for its occurrence?' does not trouble us. We can accept that there is no purpose, whether reasonable or not, behind its occurrence. However, in the case of an event which is important in our lives, we find it less comfortable to entertain the idea that there may be no reason, purpose or intention which explains (and maybe justifies) why it has happened to us. The absurdity of a random accident is hard to cope with when it has a decisive effect upon our lives or upon the life of another. The suggestion that there is no point which gives meaning to it is deeply disturbing. We find ourselves assuming that there must be a reason for it. Why did it happen? Why? Why?

Our desire to find an understandable meaning behind the individual events that have major effects on our lives is even stronger when it comes to life and reality as a whole. Is all that is the product of a random accident in a mindless quantum flux some fourteen or fifteen billion years ago? Is human being in general and are the lives of Alex and you and me and everyone else among the most recent results of chance interactions of particles without any underlying purpose? Some hold that this is the case. In their judgement, while some individual events may make sense because there is a personal purpose behind them, and while we may make sense of our own lives by our intentional activity, it is a mistake to look for some overall intention, reason or meaning in what there is. Others question this position. Theists in particular characteristically hold that behind all that exists there is an ultimate which is most adequately apprehended as personal and whose personal purposing gives meaning to reality as a whole.

Whether or not what theism maintains is rationally credible (and this book is written from the conviction that it is), it asserts what many people want to hear, namely, that in the end things really do make sense – and make sense in terms of the purposes of one who is holy, ultimate, perfect and indestructible. Part of the attractiveness of the so-called teleological arguments for the existence of God is that they purport to identify grounds for holding that there is such personal purposing underlying what we find to be the case. It is purposing which, if we could apprehend it fully, would be seen to make sense of the character of what is. In practice, however, the cases presented tend to be unconvincing because the reality of a purposive God is not so much a conclusion established by the argument as a presupposition used to guide the selection of 'evidence' for such an intentional ground of all.

Perhaps not surprisingly, most of those who believe that the purposive agency of God makes sense of the whole of reality go on to hold that particular divine intentions give specific meaning to individual events in the life of a human being. It is not enough for such believers to hold that God has a plan which gives meaning to the whole of reality. Any such meaning seems hugely remote from the experience of this or that person. There is little joy in holding that one is a drop in the ocean, especially when that 'ocean' has the dimensions of the cosmos. What is sought is a way to affirm the theistic significance of the life of each individual as a distinct person.

Sometimes attempts to affirm such significance have

ludicrous – and potentially self-defeating – results. Belief in the reality of particular providences leads some believers to hold that God has intentionally organized, and so there is a divine purpose in, the thunderstorm occurring at the vicarage garden-party, or in the breakdown of the amplification equipment in the church, or in the lecturer's sore throat! Such believers, however, usually have also to admit that in many cases they cannot even guess what that purpose may be – although they are also happy to suggest that any fortunate result of the event may be what God had had in mind (the thunderstorm forced Millicent and Cynthia to co-operate, the breakdown meant that deaf Fred did not hear the minister's appalling gaffe, the sore throat meant that we had a short lecture and could see the end of the test match on TV).

The result is ludicrous because it transforms the holy and ultimate into a fussy fiddler – and one whose actions often appear inconsistent and unfair (the thunderstorm also ruined crops, the breakdown in amplification meant that Jane, who would have giggled at the gaffe, did not hear other remarks which would have helped her to sort herself out . . .). It is potentially self-defeating because, by affirming that God controls all events, it not only entails an enormous problem of evil, it also implies that there is no significance in human being as such. If God so determines each event, the meaning of an event is the divine intention expressed in what happens. The individual constituents of the natural order and historically existing human beings are puppets manipulated by the divine. In that case it is incoherent to affirm that the loving purposing of God is that all things should have their own meaning and worth. The only reality whose actions give meaning and worth is the divine.

Bearing in mind these implications in relation to events like the vicarage garden-party and the lecturer's sore throat, the obvious solution is to hold that God does not directly control such events. There is freedom and autonomy in the created order: God does not intervene to control what happens. Such a response is widely acceptable at the level of the relatively trivial. Whether or not it rains at the vicarage tea-party, or whether or not we see the match, is not that important.

Many believers, however, do not find it a satisfactory way of responding when much more serious issues come under scrutiny. In cases like that of Alex, they want to hold that there is an underlying divine intention which not only gives meaning to what happens but also justifies it. Otherwise, they judge, events falsify their faith in the reality of God as a loving providence who is salvifically and effectively concerned for the well-being of each person.

Such believers thus assert that the condition of a handicapped person is due to the will of God. In their opinion, this must be so. Nothing, at least nothing so important as a state or an event that moulds an individual's being, can be the case unless it accords with God's purposes. If this could not be affirmed, reflection on the condition of some people would force us to accept the validity of an existentialist affirmation of the absurdity of life.

Those who assert that what occurs is according to the will of God may, nevertheless, be unable to discern the particular purposes which direct the divine will in this or that case. All that they can do, whether it contents them or not, is to locate such purposes in the inscrutability of the divine. While, therefore, they insist that there must be some purpose in what is found to be the case, they do not back their affirmation by an interpretation of the facts of the case. Instead, they expound what they consider to be required by authentic faith in God, namely, belief that everything does have a purpose because it is according to the divine will. Whatever happens must happen because God so chooses. And whatever God wills must be for the best because God is perfect.

When applied to Alex, this way of making sense of faith in God implies that his condition and what happened to him are understandable in principle, in that these things must have been in accordance with God's purposes. As such they must also be acceptable because the objects of the divine will are to be trusted to be self-justifyingly good. Unfortunately for those believers who, like Anselm, desire a faith that makes sense, a purpose which is understandable in principle and to God may not be understandable by human beings. It may be beyond our apprehension, or God may not have revealed it even though it is humanly graspable. As cartographers used to write 'Here be monsters' on 'terra incognita', so believers have to accept that many parts of the map of faith have to be inscribed 'Here be mysteries'.

There can be no doubt that many believers, faced with situations which threaten their faith in the reality of a loving God, have found comfort in such a faith. Whatever may actually occur, they trust that all is for the best according to the superintending providence of God. They thus make their own faith the conviction which Leibniz formulated when he argued that since God is by definition perfect, God must necessarily exist as the perfect creator of all, and hence the actual world must be the best of all possible worlds. Furthermore, such believers are likely to consider that only reference to the will of God is sufficient to make sense of such states as that of Alex, even though it is at the same time an 'explanation' of which they can make no material sense since its content is hidden in the mystery which is God. The faith which entertains this response is thus a fundamental trust that all is well, in spite of what may sometimes appear to be the case from our limited human appreciation of things. In biblical terms it is to take utterly seriously the text 'and God saw all that he had made, and it was very good' (Genesis 1.31). At the same time faith may offer no material answer to the question 'Why?' in a particular case: it accepts that the reasons which would show how and why this or that state of affairs is very good may be humanly unfathomable.

Underlying this response, and distorted in it, is an important insight into the content of theistic faith. It is the insight which was given to Julian of Norwich as she

> often wondered why the beginning of sin was not prevented by the great foreseeing wisdom of God; for then – or so it seemed to me – all would have been well . . . But Jesus, who in this vision informed me of all that I needed, answered with this word saying: 'Sin must needs be, but all shall be well. All shall be well; and all manner thing shall be well.' (Julian of Norwich 1980: 91)

It is a conviction which has become widely known in the twentieth century through being taken up in the closing lines of T. S. Eliot's 'Little Gidding': 'All manner of thing shall be well/When the tongues of flame are in-folded/Into the crowned knot of fire/And the fire and the rose are one.'

The significance of this insight into faith is twofold. One aspect of it is the recognition that God, the gracious, perfect and holy, is 'over all and through all and in all' (Ephesians 4.6). Everything is thus to be recognized as pervaded and embraced by the loving purposes of the divine. The other aspect is the hope that ultimately the love of God will overcome whatever spoils, distorts and destroys. Although *now* the world contains much that is imperfect, *then* all will be right. It is important to note, however, that this affirmation of the harmony of all things according to the divine vision is not an uncovering of what is actually the case at present. It is an image of a future state of affairs. The hope that it will eventually come about is an expression of confidence in the indestructible grace of God. The implied worry behind the story of Noah, namely, that humankind's evils may lead God to despair of it, reflects a human desire to start again from scratch. Closer to a valid insight into the divine is the promise at the end of the story that God will never destroy the world, whatever happens within it (cf. Genesis 9.12f).

As creator, God is to be thought of as respecting the integrity of the creation. The relationship between God and the processes of reality is accordingly to be conceived as one of mutual independence in certain respects and of inter-dependence in others.

On the one hand, God and the world are interdependent in that God is the ground of all that is and will be the ground of whatever may come to be in the future. This latter aspect of the relationship of interdependence has often been overlooked in theological understanding. While nothing can come to be that is totally independent of God, God cannot avoid being the God of whatever comes to be. As with the relationship between parent and child, so too with that between God and each being: a child's coming into being depends on the parents, but from the conception of that child the parents cannot avoid being for ever after his or her parents, whatever the child becomes or decides to do.

On the other hand, God and the world are independent so

far as both God and the active agents constituting the world have relative degrees of autonomy. God's autonomy is relative to, and so limited by, God's nature and will as the essentially perfect, holy and gracious; each creature's autonomy is limited by the extent of the freedom of choice intrinsic to its nature. The resulting understanding of the relationship between God and the world is well expressed by Whitehead when he describes God as being both the inspiration for and receptive of all the processes of reality. God's agency in affecting all that happens is not to be envisaged as the exercise of coercive force but as the 'patient', 'tender' and unceasing influence of the divine 'vision of truth, beauty, and goodness' (Whitehead 1978: 346).

The real, if limited, independence of the constituents of reality means that whatever is now the case is not necessarily as it is because God wills that it be so in that particular way. Consequently those who find comfort in holding that what seems to them pointless must have meaning in some (albeit unfathomable) divine purpose may be criticized for failing to distinguish between the creative grounding of all things in God and the divine vision of a harmony which may be actualized in the future. Not everything is as God desires. Some processes seem clearly to have resulted in states which are not in accord with God's purposes. To hold otherwise is to hold God directly responsible for the suffering, aimlessness and sin as well as the joy, fulfilment and virtue in the world. Such a being would not be an object of worship but a candidate for moral counselling!

What is important, however, is to decide which actual states are according to the divine will and which are not. Such decisions are not easy to make. In the case of people like Alex, for example, what grounds warrant holding that their basic situation is not what God wills? It is not satisfactory simply to point out that such situations are not what we would will for them. We do not share God's perspective. Consequently God's understanding of good purposes is presumably in many respects beyond our appreciation. Is it possible, then, to justify the judgement that the condition of a particular handicapped person is not what God wills – with the implication that it is a mistake for those who trust in God to believe that there is a particular divine purpose which gives meaning to the basic condition of that person? Those who find solace in such a belief may not only object that such a judgement takes away from them a way of accepting the situation while retaining their faith in a loving God. They may also challenge the judgement by arguing that it arises from a combination of lack of faith in God's providence and a presumptuous attempt to impose human understanding on the divine. How may such a charge be answered?

Those who argue about the nature and will of God should bear in mind the cautionary tale which Voltaire included in a dialogue about knowledge of the divine in his *Philosophical Dictionary*:

> I had just had a toilet built at the end of my garden, when I heard a mole arguing with a June bug: 'Here's a fine building,' said the mole. 'It must have been a pretty powerful mole who did this work.' 'You're joking,' said the June bug; 'it's a mighty talented June bug who is the architect of this building.' From that time on I resolved never to argue. (Voltaire 1962: 240)

Just as children can be funny when they are seriously imitating (what they take to be) adult behaviour, so theologians who try to expound the reality, purposes and activity of God may, at least from the divine perspective, seem hilariously pretentious. When I mentioned to Alex's mother that I was trying to write something about what he had brought me to see, she deflated my pomposity with, 'I bet he's up there laughing at you.' I hope so – although, as I will suggest later, if this be so he will be doing it in God's amusement at these efforts.

The presumptuousness of trying to judge the ways of God is powerfully expressed in the final chapters of the book of Job. After Job and his friends have tried to make sense of the divine will, God asks: 'Who is this whose ignorant words cloud my design in darkness?' (Job 38.2). Then, in a series of rhetorical questions, God points to one thing after another which is outside Job's understanding. The conclusion is that a human being is in no position to dispute about the ways of God. Job confesses:

I have spoken of great things I have not understood,
things too wonderful for me to know . . .
Therefore I melt away [*or*, despise myself];
I repent in dust and ashes. (Job 42.3, 6)

What ought we to do? It may be that our attempts to make theological sense of our experience of life and of God's intentions irritate rather than amuse the divine. Should we, like Job (cf. Job 40.3ff), shut up? When we consider the ultimacy of the divine and the finitude of the human, unquestioning acceptance may seem to be the proper stance of those who believe in God.

Such a stance is not, however, proper – nor perhaps even possible – for self-aware human beings. As Anselm suggested by the phrase *fides quaerens intellectum* (faith seeking understanding), a living faith has an inner dynamic which makes believers seek ever-fuller understanding of it. Consequently, to question faith is a mark of authentic faith, not an indication of incipient apostasy. The search for understanding, furthermore, is not an idle intellectual exercise. Although the living heart of faith is a personal relationship with the divine rather than the entertainment of certain notions as true, that relationship is unlikely to develop fruitfully if it is moulded by misleading or inadequate ideas. My relationship with John, for example, is unlikely to make much progress if I have so misinterpreted his motives that I systematically fail to understand the significance of his actions towards me. So, too, with the believer and God: wrong beliefs can so distort faith's self-understanding that the faith itself atrophies.

Finally, the view that faith in God is a matter of the unquestioning acceptance of certain ideas may be countered by the argument that such a position may be a disguised form of atheism. It is such if it absolutizes what people have previously held to be the truth about God rather than submits itself to the search for what is ultimately true. Obedient faith in God, in other words, involves a commitment to seek the truth, however disturbing, because ultimately the truth is what God is and knows. As Newman recognized, to live is to change; developments in theological understanding may accordingly be seen as the sign of a living faith in God, not the mark of error.

While, however, theological discussion may thus be defended in principle, what is important for our purposes here is its application to a particular question. What grounds, therefore, are there for holding that the condition of handicapped people like Alex is not the will of God? There are two sides to the case to be considered. On the one hand, the profound unsatisfactoriness of arguments to reconcile such human states with the will of God needs to be shown; on the other hand, it is important to give positive reasons for holding that such states are not divinely willed.

First, then, what arguments are offered to reconcile such states with the divine will, and why are they untenable? Three kinds of argument deserve to be considered, both because they appear to have some theological plausibility and because they are apparently entertained by many who profess to believe in God. Each attempts to reconcile the condition of handicapped people with the will of God. None of the arguments, however, stands up to rational examination.

One of these arguments maintains that handicaps are punishments for sin. In the case of people who are handicapped from birth, one form of this argument maintains that these people are being punished in advance for what God knows that they will do later in life. Such a suggestion is rationally unconvincing and morally abhorrent. Theologically it presupposes that God knows future contingent events and so knows what a morally responsible person (and therefore a free agent) will do in situations that have not yet occurred. Such a notion is incoherent. Whatever is to happen in the future, because of what is meant by referring to the 'future' (i.e., to what is not yet actual), is not yet determined. Hence whatever will occur in the future is essentially not knowable, not even by God (cf. Pailin 1989: 86f). Morally the argument collapses for a number of reasons. Not only does it imply that persons are morally responsible for deeds that they cannot avoid doing in the future (for they must inevitably do them if this argument is to show that the punishment is warrantable); it also attributes an unfairness to God which is deeply repellent. While handicapped people as a class may well be as morally mixed as any other group, the incidence of handicap appears to bear no defensible relationship to moral desert. It is worth noting in this respect that Jesus is recorded as rejecting the claim that those who suffer are picked on because of their sinfulness (cf. Luke 13.1ff; John 9.1ff). The same view presumably also applies to those who are handicapped.

Another form of this argument is even more morally objectionable. It maintains that handicaps are imposed on some people as punishment for the sins of others. It is, of course, clear that some people do suffer because of what others have done. Babies are born with inherited drug addiction; soldiers die because of the megalomania of rulers; passers-by are maimed by terrorist bombs. These things happen. But they are not just. What they make clear is that morality is a social as well as a personal matter. My actions are not only my individual affair: in many cases they affect others. What large groups of us do (for example, in the use of energy or in family planning) may have major consequences for the quality of life of future generations. The social significance of human behaviour, however, does not demonstrate the justice of situations in which some suffer because of the wrongs of others. In human affairs the notion that such a relationship is just is unacceptable. Whether it is children being ostracized at school because of the crimes of their father or a village being destroyed as a reprisal for guerrilla attacks, such punishment is unfair. If the source of the suffering is held to be God's activity, the notion is even more repellent. It is blasphemous to imply that God's actions resemble those of the Germans who destroyed Lidice.

Those who still hanker after a biblical basis for such a theodicy should note that the proverb about the children's teeth being set on edge because their fathers have eaten sour grapes is cited in Jeremiah and Ezekiel in order to be rejected (Jeremiah 31.29f; Ezekiel 18.1ff). What these prophets look forward to is a state where each person receives the appropriate deserts for his or her own behaviour – the Kantian *summum bonum* where virtue and happiness are exactly proportioned. As we have previously noted, this notion offers no way of reconciling the occurrence of handicaps with the divine will.

A second attempt to reconcile handicap with the will of God argues that handicaps are justifiable as tests of character. Those who put forward this argument regard life as a kind of adventure course. It contains challenges to initiative and endurance which provide opportunities for personal development. The presence of these challenges is no accident. It is according to God's will as creator.

Such a view of life's difficulties may appeal to a hearty squash-playing executive, but it may not have the same attractiveness if she finds herself paralysed, unable to play and unable to work. What is fundamentally wrong with this view, however, is not that some people are faced with severe challenges to their character. This does happen, and some people respond in admirable ways – although, it must also be recognized, others are crushed by what happens to them. What is fundamentally wrong with this view is its implied understanding of God. God is presented as behaving outrageously.

An instructor on an adventure course who knows the conditions and the skills of a group of volunteers may set them tasks which are demanding. The volunteers may find what is demanded of them very uncomfortable. The problems may stretch them and some may not cope. Some may grow through the experience; others may regress. All, furthermore, have volunteered to take part – even though some may have been persuaded by superiors who know what is good for them! This makes sense of the human behaviour that is involved. It does not provide a satisfactory analogy for thinking about the divine will for humanity.

It is not a satisfactory analogy, firstly, because handicapped people do not volunteer to face the challenges of their handicaps. Secondly, there seems to be no match between a person's potential and the demands which are made upon that person. Those who claim that divine grace is available to enable each person to overcome all problems, no matter how severe, seem to be either complacent or blind. Is a child to be expected to have the potential to cope fruitfully with being abused? Is that child to be regarded as having failed the test if later in life she or he is bitter, withdrawn and suspicious of other people? Lethargy may be deplorable, but is it likely to be avoidable by a person who has known nothing but sickness, rejection, poverty and homelessness? To maintain that everyone has the power to triumph reinforces the blindness of the falsely pious at the cost of adding to the burdens of the defeated. It is bad enough to be crushed by life; it is even worse to be told that not to have triumphed over adversity is one's own fault.

Thirdly, if the scale of the problems faced by some is divinely intended for them, the only aim for setting those problems that makes sense seems to be that of limiting rather than promoting their personal being. What enhancement of personal being is produced by handicaps that severely limit the individual's capacity for self-expression, and even more for self-awareness? To talk of challenges to be overcome is repulsive when one thinks of a massively brain-damaged baby who has survived birth, or of a middle-aged scholar who, because of brain disease, is now incapable of remembering anything that happened more than five minutes ago, or of a demented old man who wanders confusedly in the narrow world of his ward, trying to find his way to work and home. A challenge is good when it helps us to develop. The state in which some people have to exist, either because of external circumstances or because of personal characteristics, is not such a challenge. It cannot therefore be justified as a state which God wills in order to promote our development as persons.

There is, however, a variant to this argument which holds that the condition of the handicapped, especially the severely handicapped, is justified not as an opportunity for their personal development but as an opportunity for the personal development of those who care for them. This argument will be examined in more detail – and rejected – in the next chapter. Reflection shows it to be unsustainable. While it may help those who look after the handicapped to regard the demands of caring as a challenge whose conquest will enhance their own personal being, to hold that this benefit justifies the condition of those needing care is grotesque. A person who made a child suffer in order to develop the love of the parents, the ingenuity of medical researchers, the compassion of nurses and the moral outrage of by-standers would be deemed to be a monster. Similarly it would be deemed monstrous to damage a child's brain in order to challenge the skill of the child's teachers. Such judgements would be correct.

It would make no difference if the person bringing about the handicap were the ultimate and supreme reality. Such a being would not be identifiable as 'God' because such actions would show that that being is not a proper object of worship. Persons are not objects that may justifiably be used for the benefit of others. Politicians who hold that the worth of persons lies in what they can contribute to others, either to other individuals or to society in general, are as near moral bankruptcy as those who hold that worth lies in what persons can achieve for themselves.

The state of handicapped people cannot be justified by holding that it is for the good of others. To suggest that it can be so justified is to ascribe immoral purposes to the divine in a vain attempt to make sense of the senseless.

The third attempt to reconcile handicap with the will of God which we are to consider resorts to the appeal to mystery. Those who put forward this position do not start, however, by acknowledging the mysteriousness of God's nature and ways. Generally they start by arguing that there are sound reasons, whether a priori (i.e., from considering the notion of the divine) or a posteriori (i.e., from considering the actual character of the world) or both, for holding that God exists as one who is ultimate and perfect. Having shown the justification of this conclusion, apparent counter-evidence is brushed away on the grounds that it only *seems* to us to contradict the conclusion because we are not capable of comprehending things from God's perspective. The mysteriousness of the divine is thus introduced *after* the basic theistic position has supposedly been established, as a way of coping with what otherwise would have to be taken into account as counter-considerations – in some cases very strong ones.

Since, then, they are confident that it is reasonable to believe in the reality of God as a benevolent and all-controlling providence, some maintain that all things must be for the best since God must have created the best of all possible worlds. It is a position which Leibniz, for example, considered to be necessarily true. On the grounds that God, as the perfect being, must exist and be the origin of all else, he concludes not only that the world must have been created by God but also that what God has created must be the best of all possible worlds.

So far as the conclusion is held to apply to the fundamental nature of reality, it may be sustainable. Whether or not it be so depends on the cogency of its a priori argument for the reality of God. It is important to recognize, however, that all that it implies about particular actual events in the world is that the basic structure which determines the range of events which can occur is the one that overall will make possible the maximum realization of value. That structure may not prevent the occurrence of individual events which are massively harmful to particular individuals. If, for example, the maximum realization of value requires that the world contain free agents, it is arguable that their freedom must include allowing them to choose between good and evil actions. If this be so, the divine will for and creation of the best possible world cannot prevent such agents doing what is evil. When, therefore, the case of handicapped people is considered, it needs to be recognized that it does not follow that what is true of the basic character of the world in general is also to be held to be true of each event in particular. If, that is, it is reasonable to conclude that the world has been created by God as the best possible one, it does not follow that each individual event must be held to have been determined by God and so must be the best possible even though human beings may not be able to perceive in every case how this is so.

It is the application to individual events of the Leibnizian conclusion that this is the best possible world which Voltaire caricatures in the figure of Dr Pangloss in *Candide*. Observing an earthquake in which 'thirty thousand men, women and children were crushed to death under the ruins', Dr Pangloss comments that 'all this is a manifestation of the rightness of things . . . because everything is for the best' (Voltaire 1947: 33, 35). Later in the story, after having been hanged and partially dissected but, through incompetence, not killed, and having been bastinadoed and condemned to be a galley-slave, he still affirms his 'original view', namely, that 'everything in this world is for the best'. When he then asserts that he maintains his position as a philosopher, and that Leibniz with his doctrine of the pre-established harmony 'cannot be wrong' (Voltaire 1947: 136), the most convincing response seems the retort, 'So much the worse for philosophy!' If this be what pure reason demonstrates, it is not the highest wisdom but ridiculous absurdity.

Most theists, however, do not believe because they have been persuaded by an a priori argument. Their faith in the reality of God is the product of a variety of rational, empirical, experiential and cultural factors. Nevertheless, for most of them a major implication of their theistic faith is the belief that things are as they are because God, the ultimate, so wills them to be. Many of them, furthermore, apply this belief to individual events. Because they believe in God they consider that not only the basic structure of reality as a whole but also each particular event must be for the best because it is so ordained by God. It is an aspect of faith that gives believers both great confidence (because they believe that all things are in the hand of God) and also great bewilderment (because they cannot perceive why God wills certain things to happen).

This application of faith in God implies that God is responsible for the enormous cruelty that is associated with natural and moral evils. If this were so, the honest response to God would not be adoration but condemnation. Believing that all came from God, and faced with all that happened to him, should not Job have accepted his wife's advice to 'curse God and die'? His response that this is the talk of 'any wicked fool of a woman' because faith requires us to accept evil as well as good (Job 2.9f) is theologically unacceptable as well as sexist! It is unacceptable because it implies that 'God' is an ambiguous power who cannot be trusted always to act benevolently. Instead the divine seems to be understood as being like a dictator whose caprice may bring pain as easily as it may bring joy to individual subjects.

Attempts have been made to justify the unpredictable ways of God on the grounds that all belongs to God and hence that God may do whatever God wills with God's own possessions. Such a principle is unsatisfactory when applied to human possessions – and this is not just because it is arguable that we do not own anything absolutely, but only have it in trust from God. It is fundamentally unacceptable because it ascribes to owners both the rights of absolute possession and absolute rights over whatever they possess. Such a view of ownership is not morally justifiable. Even if those who possess great works of art were allowed the moral right to do as they please with what they own (e.g., remodelling a sculpture, painting a moustache on the portrait of a lady) – and this moral right is very dubious – it is certainly not morally justifiable in the case of parents and the owners of slaves. As is recognized in our culture, parents do not have absolute rights over their offspring while slave owners have no rights over their slaves. Moral sensibility demands that even those who are supposedly possessed be recognized to have rights. Their integrity and worth as persons must be appropriately respected. Furthermore, to be morally good is consistently to promote the well-being of others. Capriciously to inflict suffering is not to act in such a way. Accordingly, when the perfection and hence the moral goodness of God is combined with the recognition that to create in any case involves respect for the integrity of what is created, it becomes clear that supposed property rights do not provide a way of justifying God's responsibility for the state of handicapped people.

How, then, is the believer to reconcile faith in God as purposively controlling all that happens in the world with the actuality of some events that seem to be utterly contrary to a loving will? Whatever can be the purposes of God in allowing, let alone willing, such things to occur? A traditional answer, as has been suggested, is to resort to the appeal to mystery. Although it may not be possible to imagine what God's purposes in these events might be, faith in God is held to require believers to accept that God knows that there are perfectly good reasons for their occurrence. Faith in such matters is to accept as mystery – as good that is beyond human understanding – what cannot be made sense of as good rationally. This is the way of reconciling the presence of evil with the reality of God that is propounded by God in answer to Job's questions (cf. Job 38–41). Basically it asserts that human beings are not in a position to identify the divine purposes which make sense of individual events. Those purposes are beyond their apprehension. There are reasons, excellent reasons, for what happens. Unfortunately we are not capable of perceiving them (cf. also Isaiah 55.8).

To return to the case of Alex, such a way of reconciling his condition with the will of God is comforting and may well seem plausible. That God had a perfectly good purpose in what happened in his case (and in all other cases) is comforting because it means that there was meaning in what happened. That this purpose is beyond our grasp should not be surprising: we are human and not divine. God knows what is really good so much better than we do. The reason for what happened may thus be a mystery to us, but faith in the reality of God requires us to hold that there was a perfectly good reason for it. In this way believers consider that they can tackle the problem of how to hold that what happens in the world is according to the will of God; in difficult cases that harmony is to be affirmed even though its material nature is to be accepted as a mystery beyond any believer's grasp.

This view of faith treats it as a matter of submission and trust – 'our duty is not to understand but simply to accept'. Such a faith does not show in a credible way that the will of God is reconcilable with what happens in the world. Instead it blindly asserts that it is so – and, indeed, that it must be so. Because of this it is fundamentally flawed. This is not merely because it contradicts our humanity as thinking beings and the character of faith as 'a reasonable duty and service'. Such an objection may be challenged on the grounds that it ascribes too great a significance to human rationality. What is critically wrong with this affirmation of the mysteriousness of God as the object of faith is that it undermines faith itself. It does this because the appeal to mystery empties faith of its positive content. The reason for this is that by recognizing that we cannot understand the will of God in this and that event, we cast doubt on what we may consider to be the divine will for other events. If we appeal to mystery because we cannot make sense of the divine will *here*, can we be sure that we have correctly perceived it *there*? If some aspects of the will of God are to be held to be beyond our grasp, it may be that all are. The fact that at some points we recognize that we do not understand the will of God may thus give us reasons to think that we are deluding ourselves in other cases where we think that we have perceived the divine will. The appeal to mystery is a weapon that may turn against its user.

As Toland points out in *Christianity not Mysterious* (1696), it is not possible to believe in what does not make sense to us. It is not possible because we cannot in that case know what it is that we are supposed to be believing. I cannot, for example, believe in 'blictri' if I am totally unaware of what is meant by 'blictri'. The fact that Toland's book was ordered to be burned by the public hangman in Dublin does not make his point invalid! Those who are worried by a reference to Toland and look for support from more orthodox believers may find comfort in the fact that this is a point which Newman makes in his *Grammar of Assent*. He does this when he recognizes that apprehension is a condition of the assent of faith (cf. Newman 1985: 16 ff).

The argument that attempts to reconcile handicap with the will of God by reference to mystery thus turns out to be unhelpful. It does not give reasons to show that the two are reconcilable: it merely asserts the belief that they are reconcilable. In that case it would be more honest to admit that the appeal to mystery shows that no way can be found of reconciling them.

As was mentioned earlier, it is important to offer positive arguments for holding that the state of handicapped people is not according to the will of God as well as to show the unconvincingness of arguments which attempt to reconcile handicap with the will of God. Having therefore sought to satisfy the latter negative task by considering why arguments for reconciliation from punishment, testing and mystery do not stand up to scrutiny, it is time to consider what positive reasons may be presented for holding that handicap is contrary to the will of God. There are in the main two interrelated reasons. Both are based upon the identification of God as the ultimate ground of all reality who is the proper and totally adequate object of worship. One draws out the implications of this definitive character of the divine; the other comes from reflecting on the creative purposes of God.

The first of these arguments is that as the proper and totally adequate object of worship, God must both be intrinsically perfect and seek the highest good in others. A being that inflicted handicaps on others, either by deliberate intention or by unconcerned negligence, would fail to satisfy Anselm's definition of 'God' as 'that than which a greater cannot be conceived'. However threatening its power might be, such a being would not be the object of utterly unqualified adoration.

Rejection of this point only makes sense in terms of a perverted understanding of value which considers sadistic treatment of others to be superior to actions which promote their flourishing. Sadly it has to be admitted that some persons do seek and to some extent find a kind of satisfaction in such behaviour. They prove to themselves thereby that they have power to force others to obey their will. In this way they consider that they display their importance. Thus we find parents who cow their children, older children who bully younger ones, thugs who threaten weaklings, and adults who mistreat infirm parents. Similar things occur in relationships between social groups. These patterns of behaviour are not, however, admirable. They are sad as well as disgusting. Those who find satisfaction because they think that they assert their worth in such ways are deluded. What they display are their inadequacies. They are not to be praised but pitied; they need help to find the true worth of their being.

Analogously, to think of God as affirming the divine worth by the exercise of irresistible power is to think of God in terms of the worst rather than of the best of what we know in human being. It is, furthermore, theistically incredible to conceive of God as being so unsure of the divine worth as to want to show off by giving and withholding in arbitrary ways. When, as has too often happened in the past, believers and theologians have thought of God as acting in such ways, they have made petty-minded tyrants their model for the divine. By fashioning their concept of God on the lowest rather than on the highest modes of behaviour, they have not glorified God but insulted the divine. There are no inadequacies in the divine, let alone any which entrap God in the error of seeking compensation by oppressing others.

If it is still not obvious that the essential perfection of the divine is incompatible with willing that some people be more handicapped than others, and that some be enormously handicapped, it is hard to see what further arguments can be presented. Perhaps all that can be done is to illustrate the point until it is perceived to be self-evidently true. Consider, therefore, particular cases of those who are generally regarded as handicapped persons; consider especially the individual states of those who are severely handicapped; compare their states with the position of those who are not restricted in these ways, at least not to anything like the same degree. Then consider the notion that the handicapped people are as they are because 'God' deliberately wills that this is how each of them should be. Now try to worship that being. It is impossible – at least this is what I find.

To make the point particular, if I believed that Alex's problems were what 'God' desired for him and for those that loved him, I would have only one honest response – to condemn that 'God'. Such a being would not be the loving one who elicits adoration. It would be a brute whose behaviour is to be condemned. Those who think otherwise, and so would find it possible to adore such a being, have a sense of value which I cannot even imagine, let alone agree with. As for those who may try to reject this case on the grounds that it appeals to the emotions rather than to reason, my response is that their comment indicates to me that they have failed to understand (or are trying to hide from) what the argument is about.

Some acts are evil. It is not justifiable to will them. They are, therefore, not coherently attributable to God's will. To will handicap is one of them.

The other positive argument for denying that God deliberately wills that some people be handicapped can be dealt with more briefly. It is the argument that such a will would contradict the divine intention as creator. As will be suggested in the discussion of the problem of evil in chapter seven, it is difficult to give material content to the notion of divine creativity. Nevertheless, in whatever way God as creator is to be held to influence the course of events, it is incoherent to hold that this would include handicapping people.

Since God is intrinsically perfect, divine activity must be motivated by the highest good. Accordingly it must aim at the realization of the fullest experiences of joy and aesthetic delight since these are the experiences of what is good in itself. Such experiences, furthermore, are not to be envisaged as belonging to the divine in a restricted way. Just as the previous argument holds that the divine perfection means that God is not to be thought of as a person who bullies to hide doubts about self-worth, so this argument holds that God is not to be thought of by analogy with a selfish art-collector who gloats over a private collection and finds no pleasure in what others can share. On the contrary, the divine is not inhibited by envy or limited by possessiveness.

As the panentheistic concept of the divine makes clear (cf. Pailin 1989: chapter 5), God's outgoing love means that all experiences are experienced by God. God has joy in sharing the positive values of others' experiences as well as pain in sharing their hurts. In the former respect the enrichment that parents receive from observing their children is a model for understanding the attitude of the divine as creator to the world as created. Parents, at least good ones, do not resent the attainments of their children: they find joy in their children's joys. Whether it is a little girl announcing proudly to her mother, 'I blewed it out' after puffing at a candle, or a toddler intently observing a worm, or whether the 'children' are adults enjoying much more sophisticated pleasures, part of the pleasure of those who love them is found in empathizing with them and so in sharing their enjoyments. Even more is this true of God as the one whose love is tinged by no selfishness whatsoever and whose empathy is totally unrestricted. The conspiratorial smiles of grandparent and grandchild after having enjoyed a secret treat of which too-sensible parents would disapprove may be even closer to the divine joy in sharing our delights!

If, then, we take seriously the doctrine that God, as the one whose nature is revealed in Jesus as 'the man for others', is one whose love is total and whose awareness is unrestricted, it follows that it is nonsensical to ascribe to divine creativity any will to restrict the potential experiences of others. The opposite must be the case. Not because God seeks to gain from sharing those experiences (although God does so gain) but because God loves, God's creative will must be that all enjoy in their own ways the richest and broadest experiences of living. Furthermore, whereas parents in clumsy attempts to do the best for their child may try to impose their own goals in life upon their child, God respects the integrity of each person. This is part of what is implied by conceiving of God as creator. God is not a puppeteer who totally controls all that happens. As the creator, God enjoys the surprises, excitements and enrichments that come from embracing the autonomous discoveries of the created.

What, then, has faith in God to affirm about handicap? It is that God does not will that any person be handicapped. There is no divine intention that gives meaning to such a state. It is not to be explained away, but responded to. Believers and theologians should apply to their views on handicapped people what Marx said about philosophers: 'The philosophers have only *interpreted* the world in various ways: the point, however, is to *change* it' (Marx 1957: 72).

The root idea in the notion of 'salvation' is that of health and healing. Accordingly, healing may be seen as a sacrament of the divine activity, and healers as among the priests who mediate and realize the divine will. So far as handicapped people are concerned, those who enable them to experience and enjoy as much as possible the fullness of life are the priests of God to them, and what they do is a sacrament of the divine. Alex's mother thus expressed God's will as well as his parents' in a comment which she made when he was only a few days old: 'We intend that he shall have as full a life as he can.' The same is the divine will for every person. According to John's Gospel, Jesus stated that 'I have come that people may have life, and may have it in all its fullness' (John 10.10). When Christians think about those who are handicapped, they must apply to them their faith that the Jesus who made this remark is the one in whom the nature and will of God are normatively perceived.

In spite of the above discussion, it may still be asked why God permits some people to be severely handicapped if such states are contrary to the divine will. This question will be discussed more fully in relation to the problem of suffering in chapter seven. Basically the answer, so far as it is an answer rather than a denial that the question is a coherent one, is that while all people (as are all actualities other than God) are finite, some are much more handicapped than others because of accidents and because of inaccuracies in the genetic process. Some of these arise from the risk that attaches to being morally responsible and so relatively free persons in a generally stable world. Others are the result of the natural order not being so completely regular that changes cannot occur in it. The chance alterations that on rare occasions lead to evolutionary developments on other occasions produce the states which we identify as handicaps. Nevertheless, no specific alteration is specifically and deliberately willed by God.

What this implies is humbling for human pretentiousness. Just as God did not will Alex to be as he was, so God did not will that the cosmic processes should result in the emergence of the particular form of self-conscious being that we know as humankind, let alone that they should result in the existence of you and me. Whatever has emerged, and whatever may emerge in the future, finds its ultimate significance, however, in being embraced by the divine.

5

The worth of persons is in the love of others for them

In a culture where the value of persons is widely judged in terms of what they contribute, the worth of severely handicapped people may well be regarded as rather low. What, it may be asked, do they add to the common good, whether that good is measured in economic terms as units of the gross national product or in terms of less tangible forms of enrichment of life in the community? Bearing in mind the demands of care, do they on balance add anything, or is their net effect to take more than they contribute?

The harsh materialism underlying these questions may not normally be presented in such a stark way, but this does not mean that such considerations do not exert a powerful, if often unacknowledged, influence on the values and attitudes of many people. While individuals and the social institutions which they endorse stress the importance of individual love and community care, there is frequently a huge gap between what is professed and what actually happens. Attractive ideals are abused when their assertion is used as a mask to cover failure to give actual care and to support it with proper funding. Individual and social life is thus stained in many places by hypocrisy, even though in many cases it is also largely unconscious.

This description of current social behaviour is not, however, universally valid. There are cases of caring and giving which are awesome in their generosity. Families in particular often make enormous sacrifices for the well-being of severely handicapped members. Nevertheless, in view of the prevailing dominance of secular materialism in contemporary culture, I was not surprised to hear the following three remarks. A smartly turned out (and apparently successful) young man in a wine bar in the City of London told an interviewer for a recent television programme that he regarded all people over fifty as wasting assets and most old people as having 'negative asset value'. They took from the community more than they put into it. According to the principle by which he judged, he was probably correct – even if, in view of his own inevitable aging, short-sighted! The net 'deficit' incurred by caring for some people is enormous when account is taken of the cost to the health and social services as well as of the wear and tear on their relatives and friends.

If the above comments seem to be the thoughtless response of a brash and insensitive yuppy, the second remark is not so readily dismissible as pagan ignorance. It comes from a person regularly attending a university chaplaincy. When a doctoral student from a Third-World country arrived with a massively handicapped toddler, the reaction of a fellow communicant was, 'Why did they let her into this country? She is going to cost this country far more than her fees are worth.' The third remark came from a doctor whose patient I do not hope to be in my old age. Talking of an old man who had recently been resuscitated after cardiac arrest, he said, 'I don't know why they bothered. He really isn't going to be much use in the future.'

While it would be unjustifiable to make much of three accidental remarks, especially without discussing their individual settings, they illustrate an attitude that is more widespread in society today than we may like to admit. Indeed, what may be most surprising about the remarks is not that these thoughts were entertained but that they were openly expressed.

One reason why such remarks are not heard more frequently may be a form of cowardice. Most people do not want to upset those who need their help, especially those who naturally look to them for support because of social ties. They would upset their dependants if they expressed such views and this would make relations with those dependants even more fraught. Another reason may be conscious or unconscious hypocrisy. Many people profess principles which are contrary to such attitudes even though what they do shows that their lives are largely moulded by them.

Although a creditable reason why such remarks are not heard more often would be that people on the whole are not in fact pretending when they assert that they do not agree with them, it was noteworthy that those who made the remarks did not appear to be at all embarrassed by them. This suggests that they were not consciously aware that the basis of their judgements might be considered to be morally questionable. In this they were, regrettably, probably typical of many people.

This lack of awareness, however, may not be simply the product of blinkered selfishness. It may also be partially explicable as the result of a confusion in moral judgement. Justified moral indignation about the selfishness of some who take aid does not justify selfishness on the part of those who refuse to give aid to persons who need it. It is one thing to be hostile to 'scroungers' who choose to get from others rather than to fend for themselves, who always seek to acquire and never give, who exploit their welfare 'rights' in society but never recognize their duties to society, who fasten like leeches on the body of the community, sucking from it as many goods as they can while admitting no obligation to contribute anything to the common wealth. Antipathy to able-bodied shirkers is not only to be expected from those who provide what they take, it is also morally justifiable. It is quite another thing, however, to fail to respond to people who have authentic needs and cannot meet them. The selfishness of those who are not justified in seeking aid does not justify the selfishness of those who refrain from giving aid to those who need it. In both cases love is strangled by self-interest.

Nevertheless, selfishness in both these forms is one of the unhappy by-products (and, according to some analysts, inescapable by-products) of a consumer society which gives high value to possession, attainment, personal freedom, and individual satisfaction. The amoral attitude of an unsocialized two year old whose most important utterances are 'mine' and 'I want' too often becomes the underlying principle of political policy, economic development and what is alleged to be social progress, adopted by people whose manifest immorality therein cannot be excused as the amorality of a toddler.

How are these remarks about the immorality of widespread social attitudes relevant to reflection on the nature of human being in the light of the state of severely handicapped people? They are relevant in two ways. In the first place, this way of valuing human beings causes deep unhappiness among those who are handicapped. Although some are happily unaware of this way of valuing personal worth, others are embarrassed by it. This is because they are aware of themselves as being net receivers from, rather than as net contributors to, the common wealth. Knowing that they are incapable of satisfying the call to 'stand on your own two feet', and remembering how the story of Captain Oates on Scott's last expedition is presented as exemplary heroism, some are troubled about what they ought to do. Secondly, those who care for the handicapped are sometimes misled by this view of the worth of persons into thinking that they need to establish the worth of handicapped people by demonstrating that they do have important contributions to make to society.

In the remainder of this chapter, we will respond to these issues by investigating what fundamentally constitutes the worth of a person, and particularly the worth of a severely handicapped person. Initially we will consider an attempt to satisfy the contributory norm of human worth which maintains that handicapped persons are in fact contributors to the good of society. After criticizing this case on several grounds, we shall then argue that the view of worth underlying the contributory norm is mistaken. The fundamental worth of each human being – and indeed of everything that exists – lies neither in what a person achieves nor in what a person makes possible for others to achieve, but in God's love for that person.

In thinking about people who are severely handicapped, it is important to distinguish between what may occur as a result of their conditions and the question of whether or not such conditions can be held in any scheme of things to be worthwhile. The fact that the condition of a severely handicapped person may have some good by-products does not make it tolerable, let alone desirable. For example, people who become blind may find in consequence that they become increasingly sensitive to sound and smell. To maintain, however, that the enhancement of some senses can compensate for, let alone justify, the loss of another is

generally not a convincing argument. It might be plausible in
some cases of relatively minor or temporary limitations –
such as in the case of tone-deafness which prevents me
being distracted by the discordant notes of a child learning
to play the violin or in the case of a sprained wrist which, by
preventing me from writing, leads me to discover the riches
of an art gallery. These, however, are trivial matters when
compared to the situation of severely handicapped people. In
their cases any balancing of costs against benefits shows
that the price of any supposed benefits is intolerable.

Because handicaps generally cannot be justified on the
grounds that they have beneficial consequences for the
handicapped persons which outweigh their costs to them,
attempts are sometimes made to argue that the cost-benefit
analysis must be done in terms of the community as a whole
rather than by considering only the situation of each
handicapped individual taken on his or her own. While
particular handicapped individuals may correctly judge the
price of any supposed benefits to them which arise from
their handicaps to be outrageous, and while some may
reasonably argue that their condition produces no benefits to
them at all, it may be argued (probably by the non-
handicapped) that the condition of handicapped people
contributes something to the general good that would
otherwise be impossible. Consequently, on the ground of
society's well-being, the states of handicapped people may be
claimed to have value since they contribute, albeit
inadvertently and unwilledly to the public good. It may thus
be concluded that handicapped people meet the challenge of
the contributory norm of worth. They, too, have a part in
increasing the common wealth.

This conclusion is justified on the grounds that
handicapped people have value because they challenge, and
perhaps even inspire, others to care for them. According,
then, to the argument which I want to examine, handicapped
persons have worth because they give others opportunities to
actualize qualities such as love, patience, tenderness,
generosity, and understanding.

An example of the kind of argument that may be put
forward is a response that was made to a patient in hospital.
He was waiting for an operation and commented to a friend

that if things went wrong, he would not want to be resuscitated if it meant that thereafter he would not only be a burden to others but also unable to live creatively. His friend replied, 'But you should not deprive others of opportunities to show their care for you.' The patient was not convinced. While he appreciated that his friends might well be willing to care for him, he argued that the fact that his condition would give others opportunities to love did not morally justify rejecting his wishes. As he put it, 'There are always plenty of others who need care. It would be no justification of my continued existence in such a state that I thereby provide others with opportunities to meet the demands which my condition makes upon them.'

In fact the operation was trouble free and so the question of 'pulling the plug' did not arise. However, was the patient's wish justified? Contemplating the demands which his continued existence might make upon others in certain circumstances, was he right to think that it would be good in such circumstances to emulate Captain Oates?

For some people it is a matter of principle that human life is sacred. On this basis they conclude that it can never be justifiable to end it, not even for the person whose life it is. However, those who maintain this principle cannot justify it by reference to Jesus if he is correctly reported as saying that he came to give his life for others (cf. Mark 10.45; John 10.11–18). Where a person has enjoyed years of self-conscious autonomy and can form rational wishes about her or his future, a decision to copy Captain Oates may be defended by powerful arguments. Leaving aside cases where a person may consider that providing an opportunity to care cannot warrant the pains to be borne (and how far should others who will not have to bear those pains presume to query this conclusion?), a person may reasonably argue that he or she loves those who would have to bear the burden of care too much to permit them to ruin their lives in caring for the fag-end of his or her own existence. In extreme cases where, as with Captain Oates, caring for one member will probably result in the destruction of the group, a decision by that member to give up his or her life is a judgement which may even be regarded as a praiseworthy application of the text that 'There is no greater love than this, that a man should lay down his life for his friends' (John 15.13). As the circumstances become less extreme, however, what is justifiable becomes less easy to determine. How should we endorse a person's unwillingness to continue in a dependent state and so as an object of others' care, and at what point should we reject it as the result of pride which needs to be replaced by the humility of accepting help from others? Nevertheless, even though the factors in individual cases are often so complex and obscure that it is hard to see where the line should be drawn, for many people the extreme cases present no problem.

An important as well as a complicating factor in making decisions about these matters is that the feelings of the carers as well as of the cared-for need to be considered. Although the demands which a person makes upon others may seem to outsiders to be enormous, in some cases those who care for that person may rightly respond that their love is far greater than the burden placed upon them. After a month at university a student told me that she was 'homesick' – for the old people for whom she had been helping to care in the previous year. For all their awkwardness, she found delight in being with them. In other cases, the story is sadly different. Caring for some imposes pressures which squeeze the delight out of life: like soggy rags the carers survive from one over-burdened day to another, afraid to admit, even to themselves, that relief may come only with the death of the ones whom they feel that they must love.

The discussion so far has focused on the case of persons who want to decide about their future existence and are rationally and morally competent to do so. In reaching their decision such people need to consider not only what in certain circumstances would be likely to be the quality of their future existence and its effects upon others, but also how those who might otherwise have to care for them might feel if they left them with a sign that they thought that their carers' love might not survive such testing.

It is important to recognize, however, that discussions about the tolerability of one's future existence and about the justifiability of the demands which it might make upon the lives of others are discussions about the quality of life. Texts about laying down one's life for others challenge Christians to take seriously the cost of discipleship. In some cases it may be necessary to face the practical implications of Jesus' description of discipleship as a matter of 'taking up the cross' (cf. Mark 8.34). A few years after Dietrich Bonhoeffer wrote that 'The cross is laid on every Christian . . . When Christ calls a man, he bids him come and die' (1959: 79), he had to realize it in his own experience.

Nevertheless, while self-sacrificial love of others is awesome, admirable and challenging, there must be no confusion between thinking about the quality of a human life and understanding the nature of its fundamental worth. The value of a human life is determined neither by the quality of its experiences nor by the richness of the experiences which it may make possible for others. Consequently reference to the quality of life does not provide a way to establish the worth of a human being.

This point needs to be insisted on when misguided attempts are made to affirm the worth of a human being by identifying what that person may make possible in the quality of the lives of others. It is particularly important to appreciate it when it is applied to the case of severely handicapped people. Unlike the patient in hospital, many such people have never been and never will be without their handicaps. They always have been and always will be to some extent dependent on others. Furthermore, unless there are enormous developments in the examination and genetic repair of fertilized eggs (and this is a prospect which, if it became feasible, would be morally controversial), there will, as Jesus said of the poor, always be such people in the community (cf. Matthew 26.11; John 12.8). Nevertheless, it has been argued, on the basis of the contributory norm of human worth, that while severely handicapped people may demand a lot of care from others, they have worth in that they make it possible for others to actualize certain values through caring for them. Their contributory place in humankind is thus held to be established on the grounds that they have an indispensable role in providing less handicapped people with challenges to care and, in actually caring, to develop the carers' personal qualities.

If, for example, the contributory norm of worth is accepted, attempts may be made to affirm the worth of severely handicapped people by applying the principle that it is good for an individual to develop her or his personal being to the full. In the light of Jesus' parable of the use of capital (Matthew 25.14ff; Luke 19.11ff), this principle may be held to express a religious as well as a moral duty. There are many different ways to satisfy it. Some people take up chess to sharpen their wits; some tackle obstacle courses to advance their physical skills; some find that preserving delicate antiques develops an attitude of patient care; while others discover that attendance at the theatre stimulates their emotional responsiveness. Along similar lines it may be pointed out that severely handicapped people present opportunities for personal development in those who care for them. The mental skills of doctors, medical researchers and technologists are challenged as they seek to heal and to alleviate handicaps and to prevent them occurring in the future; the physical abilities of those who tend severely handicapped people are often severely tested; looking after their well-being frequently draws out high levels of patience and empathy; involvement with them can be a powerful stimulus to one's emotions . . .

In a society whose values are determined by the contributory notion of human worth, it could thus be argued that severely handicapped people have worth because of the opportunities that they provide for personal growth in others. On the social level, it might be maintained that the community would be impoverished if it did not have the opportunity to face the challenges posed by severely handicapped persons among its members. It might even be argued on an individual level that a person who seeks development does not need to turn to chess, obstacle courses, antique collecting and theatre: a great variety of demanding challenges can be found in taking up care for a severely handicapped person. If imagination be allowed to run wild, it is even possible to conceive of advertisements pointing out the benefits which individuals may find in taking up such caring. It would be a message supported by those in politics whose basic concern is to reduce the taxation burden, and by preachers who consider that their proclamation of the Christian faith can only be effective if it contradicts itself by pandering to the selfishness of their hearers! Nevertheless, whether claims about benefits are justified or illusory (and a survey of carers might well provide empirical evidence which conflicts with the rhetoric about the alleged benefits), any attempt to establish the worth of handicapped people along such lines is unacceptable in principle. It is to be rejected on three counts.

In the first place, such an evaluation overlooks the fundamental point that a handicapped individual is a person. Instead of beginning from a position of respect for the dignity of the individual, this mode of evaluation starts from the position that what is primarily significant about people is their usefulness for others. Because severely handicapped people provide others who are relatively autonomous and independent with opportunities to care for them, they thus satisfy the contributory norm of worth. They are valuable, not for what they are and do, but for what they make possible for others to be and to do. In a totally passive way they provide others with a means of enhancing their existence.

This way of establishing the worth of severely handicapped people implies that if humankind were to be wiped out by plague and the last tormented survivor were severely handicapped, that person would have no value. With no one left to care about that person's well-being, she or he would be as worthless as a pebble on a beach which no one has ever noticed.

This uncomfortable implication is not, however, what is fundamentally wrong with the contributory principle for evaluating worth. This emerges from another of its implications. This is the implication that a person as an individual is not significant; what is significant about a person is what she or he contributes in one way or another to the enhancement of the lives of other people. To be valued in these terms, however, is to be depersonalized. In the case of severely handicapped people, furthermore, the contributory principle of human worth, by viewing them primarily as objects for care, endorses a demeaning and patronizing attitude towards them. They are to be treated as objects (as indeed must all people according to this principle), even if complex and sometimes unpredictable objects, to which one seeks 'to do good' – as if they were engines that need regular fuelling and cleaning, or delicate manuscripts that need to be handled with care. Valued by what they offer to the public good, they are neither given the dignity appropriate to every human being as a person for whom God cares nor seen as individuals having feelings and desires of their own, with whom the primary mode of relationship must be the 'I–thou' encounter of person to person, however hard their handicaps may make it to establish such relationships with them.

While all human beings are interdependent, nearly all are able to establish their individuality as persons by free, creative actions. Although their awareness of their environment and their capacity for autonomy may be limited, with extremely rare exceptions the most severely handicapped people, so long as they are conscious, have distinct characters. Their individuality is manifested in responses to situations and may develop through exposure to new experiences. Some like curry, others do not; some are stimulated by rock music, others prefer Mozart . . . Even those individuals who are incapable of showing personal responses may still have their own feelings; they are persons and should be treated accordingly. The basic error of valuing people by their contributory worth is that it fails to recognize the personhood of those who are so valued. By treating their worth in terms of units of significance for others, it dehumanizes them. Consequently, rather than providing a way of establishing the worth of severely handicapped people, the notion that their worth lies in what they contribute as challenges to others' care fundamentally disvalues them – as indeed it disvalues all persons to whom it is applied.

The attempt to value severely handicapped people as challenges to others' care is to be rejected, secondly, because it degrades those who care as well as those who are valued as objects of their care. Cynics whose interpretation of conduct is governed by the regulative principle that people act only out of self-interest will, of course, never be persuaded otherwise because they cannot entertain the reality of any other motivation. The assumption of this regulative principle, however, does not make the resulting interpretation true in every respect in every case. On reflection it appears to be important to distinguish the reasons why people care from the effects of caring upon them. Both are also to be seen to be complex.

There are many reasons why people care for others. Some clearly enjoy it. For others it is a matter of consciously fulfilling family or more general social obligations. The job has to be done and, whether they like it or not, they are the ones in a position to do it. Some may even engage in caring quite deliberately as a kind of character training: parents, for example, may encourage a teenager to do voluntary work in a hospital in order to counter self-centredness; young adults may volunteer to work for a while in an aid organization in order to learn to cope with a tougher style of life than they have faced hitherto. These motivations should not be despised. Others are not admirable. They include showing off (which was condemned by Jesus; cf. Matthew 6.2ff), working one's passage to heaven (which, as Luther came to realize, is self-contradictory since it is a matter of pretending to love while in reality being motivated by selfish ends), and pleasure in exercising power over others.

In many cases, however, carers would be surprised to be asked why they are concerned about those for whom they care. It would seem self-evident to them: those for whom they care need care. That is the only explanation they can give for what they do. There is no *reason* for their caring in the sense that their actions are directed by an end that is other than that of caring for the well-being of those for whom they care. They thus see their actions as self-justifying. Indeed, the motives some may ascribe to their behaviour may well be rationalizations produced by attempting to find an answer for a question whose presupposition is mistaken (namely, that there is an ulterior reason for what they do). If their actions need understanding, it is because those who are puzzled by them have not understood that love is a self-justifying and all-sufficient ground for certain kinds of behaviour. Those who remain puzzled by love (and even cynical about references to it) should therefore consider whether the contributory worth notion of value has blinded them to what is good in itself.

To ask some parents, for example, what they expect to get out of caring for their child is mistaken as well as insensitive.

This is not because parenting is to be understood wholly in biological terms as the perpetuation of the selfish gene. Even though the strength of biologically grounded instincts should not be overlooked, as self-conscious persons some parents accept responsibility for their behaviour. What is wrong with asking them what they expect to get out of caring for their child is that it is a question which is fundamentally *mal posée*. They do not expect to get anything back. Those who suggest, for example, that parents see their child as an insurance policy against the needs of their old age are not only attributing to the parents a lack of realism about social movements in current society, they do not understand what is meant by love.

To hold that care is not undertaken *for the sake of* reward does not mean that it may not be beneficial for the carer. While its demands may be enormous, for many the experience of caring brings great rewards. In caring they enhance their being. They share the joys of handicapped persons in discovering new experiences. Harsh experiences teach them about human existence and make them fuller persons. Finding that they are of use to others develops their self-respect and, less happily, their sense of self-importance. Caring may give them a satisfying sense of duty fulfilled.

On the other hand, these effects are only part of the story. Caring can be utterly exhausting and frustrating. Looking after a senile spouse can be physically, emotionally and mentally destructive. Providing a home for a disturbed adolescent can threaten the survival of that home. Bringing up a severely handicapped child can be enormously costly, not just financially but in the quality of life that remains possible for the family. It is easy for those on whom care does not lay huge burdens to speak glowingly of the sacrifices of those on whom it does. They might not see the situation in such a rosy light if night after night they had to clean the incontinent, and day after day to share their lives with those with whom intelligent, let alone lively, conversation is impossible.

Nevertheless, whatever beneficial results caring may have for some carers, it is a mistake to consider that the possibility of those results justifies the need for care and hence establishes the contributory worth of those who are cared for. The most important of those results occur as accidental by-products of the caring. They are not realized if they are its intentional goal. To decide to love in order to enjoy the benefits of loving is not to love. The benefits of loving, whatever they may be, only come to those who love for the sake of loving. Furthermore, to hold that people care for what they will get out of it is to treat carers as selfish manipulators of others. Even more obnoxious is the suggestion that those who care would regard those for whom they care as having worth because they make possible caring, and hence its fruits, for the carers.

If, after all this, love still needs to be 'explained', it is explicable as an intrinsic demand in the experience of being loved. Those who know themselves as loved do not feel burdened by a moral obligation to love others. They are driven by their own experience of love to be loving. And, accidentally rather than intentionally, they find that their experience becomes richer by sharing it with others. Love is that kind of reality. Furthermore, it is arguable that since God, the embracing ground of all being, is love, the experience of being loved is not totally absent from those who have not experienced being loved by other human beings. Although such people may not be conscious of it, love is the divine context in which all being occurs. Hence it may be held to be natural for people to love because it is the appropriate response to the fundamental character of being itself. It is not behaviour which has to be explained.

For Christians the experience of love as the reason for loving others is expressed in a hymn of Francis Xavier:

> My God, I love thee – not because
> I hope for heaven thereby,
> Nor yet because who love thee not
> Are lost eternally.

> Thou, O my Jesus, thou didst me
> Upon the cross embrace . . .
> Then, why, O blesséd Jesus Christ,
> Should I not love thee well?

> Not with the hope of gaining aught,
> Not seeking a reward:
> But as thyself hast lovéd me,
> O ever-loving Lord!

To love God, however, is to love all those whom God loves – which is to love all. This is the insight into reconciliation eventually reached by the Ancient Mariner. Becalmed 'upon the rotting sea', alone and cursed by his dead companions, 'so lonely 'twas, that God himself/Scarce seeméd there to be', he looks at the water-snakes with 'their rich attire' of 'blue, glossy green and velvet black' moving 'in tracks of shining white' that flash with 'golden fire':

> O happy living things! no tongue
> Their beauty might declare:
> A spring of love gushed from my heart,
> And I blessed them unaware.

And as thus he prays, he is freed:

> The Albatross fell off, and sank
> Like lead into the sea.

What has he learned? His tale ends with this comment:

> He prayeth well, who loveth well
> Both man and bird and beast.

> He prayeth best, who loveth best
> All things both great and small;
> For the dear God who loveth us,
> He made and loveth all.

> (Coleridge 1912: 197f, 208f)

Those who see the worth of individuals in what they contribute to the well-being of others and who suggest that carers are motivated by what they can get from their caring are ignorant of the nature of authentic love. While it is a mistake to deny that those who love sometimes find that their love brings them great satisfaction (and also at times great pain and exhaustion), it is equally a mistake to consider that this accidental by-product of their actions is the reason for them. So to interpret their behaviour is in effect to deny that they love. It is to malign their actions and to demean their relationships with those for whom they care. Furthermore, any who think that they love when they are in reality motivated by self-interest find that their motivation prevents them finding the satisfaction that attends genuine loving.

When, therefore, the contributory norm of value is not only used to misinterpret love but is also then treated as the basis of the worth of those, such as severely handicapped people, who are the recipients of apparently loving care, the error grows. The worth of those who are cared for, and also the worth of those who care, does not lie in the fruits of caring in the carers. It lies in being loved.

We will return to the question of the nature of the authentic worth of people later in this chapter. In the meantime there is a third objection to the use of a contributory norm of value to establish the worth of handicapped people. That it can be dealt with briefly does not lessen its weight. This objection points to the bizarre implications of the notion that severely handicapped people have worth because of the ways in which they enable the lives of others to be challenged and enriched. If generalized, this position could be used to justify the need for disease, despair, decay and destruction on the grounds that, if these states did not occur, there would be no opportunity for nurses and doctors, psychiatrists and therapists to develop their skills. The fact that hospitals are places where care is shown does not, however, justify the conditions that make them necessary. It would be bizarre, if not perverted and sadistic, to maintain that disease and pain are warranted because human existence would be the poorer if hospitals could be abolished and all doctors and nurses dismissed because they had nothing to do. Likewise it would be appallingly insensitive to hold that mental breakdowns and psychological traumata are worthwhile because they test the patience and insights of counsellors to the limit. Anyone who doubts this should ask those who suffer deeply what they think. Unless they are masochists (and so need help anyway), they are not likely to consider that the opportunities for developing and practising skills which their conditions provide for those who treat them make those conditions worthwhile.

Similar considerations apply to the case of severely handicapped people. Those who are not convinced should consider what would be the case if one generalized the position that the condition of handicapped people is justified because their needs provide others with opportunities for love. If this were maintained as a principle, it would presumably follow not only that the greater the needs, the greater the opportunities for responding to them, but also that the greater the needs, the more justified they are. To this those who understand the nature of divine love must respond 'God forbid' – as Paul said to those who thought that they should remain sinners in order that divine grace might be shown all the more (cf. Romans 6.2). To seek to justify handicaps in this way would be to hold that the more intractable the disease, the deeper the despair, the more threatening the decay, and the wider the destruction, the more worthwhile it is. If this is not a *reductio ad absurdum*, I do not know what one is! The worth of handicapped people is not to be justified in this way.

That the worth of handicapped people is not to be established by finding some contributory value in their need of help does not mean that such persons are not to be helped. What is mistaken is to hold that their need of support in any way justifies their state or establishes their worth as members of the human community. They are persons in their own right. Although each person develops as a person through interaction with fellow human beings, no one should be thought of merely as an adjunct to the personal development of others.

Just as to hold this is not in any way to suggest that those who are handicapped do not need support, so also it is not to question the obligation to supply it. At least for Christian understanding, there is a moral duty on those members of society who are able to do so to act, both corporately and individually, to help the disadvantaged to enjoy as full an experience of life as is feasible. To put this principle into practice, however, demands solutions to several hard questions.

Not everything that is possible is feasible. Even though the present provision of support may be judged to be disproportionately small in relation to what is potentially available (and what would be a fair proportion is not easy to determine), the total resources of the community are limited. Hence those responsible for distributing them have to seek an unhappy balance between meeting the needs of individuals and respecting the quality of life of the members of the community as a whole. For example, even if there were enough wealth in society to make available all the resources that medical science could use to prolong each human life as long as is technically possible (and there is not in fact such wealth), any attempt to make it so available would impose destructive costs upon the society seeking to provide it. Similarly, parents with a severely handicapped child have to try to find a way of balancing the demands which caring for that child makes upon them with the welfare of the other members of the family – including their own. Finding such balances is agonizing; those who have to make the decisions deserve much sympathy.

Another hard question is that of deciding how far handicapped people ought to be helped and how far they should be left to struggle for themselves. Human experience of the processes of reality suggests that God is not a maker who controls every event, but a creator who 'lets be' what comes into being, respecting and encouraging each creature's autonomous creativity. The appropriate model for the divine–human relationship is not, in that case, that of a puppeteer who determines what occurs according to what the puppeteer considers to be best. It is that of parents who encourage their children to grow in their own ways and who cherish them as the persons which they become. Furthermore, the practice of theistic faith is generally considered to require that the way in which God cares for us should be the pattern for our care for each other (cf. 1 John 4.11). This includes the pattern for the care of those who are severely handicapped.

Here again the principle that should guide decisions is easy to state but often hard to apply and painful to implement. The principle is that handicapped people should, as far as is reasonable, be given the dignity of personal independence. But what in practice is 'reasonable' and what is not? Judgements differ. Looking on from the outside it is hard to perceive the proper balance which results in help that is appropriate while avoiding depersonalizing inter-ference, however kindly its intention. Those who are actually involved in caring need great sensitivity. On the one hand, they must adjust their desire to help to the right of handicapped people to be left to their own devices. On the other, they must temper their responses to the requests of those who are handicapped by the need to encourage them, even to compel them, to discover what they can do for themselves.

In practice the borders between benign neglect and careless apathy and between fussy protection and caring aid are difficult to determine. Each case has to be treated individually, and the personal interactions between those involved complicate the decisions. Whether we think of a mother who has to decide how to respond to her crying baby or of a person who has to decide how to respond to a senile parent's wishes, of a social worker concerned about a client's self-neglect or of a therapist worried about pent-up violence in a possibly psychopathic patient, it is often puzzling to know what it is to care for a person. The best will in the world is not enough. Analysis of the likely outcomes of different responses, balancing of the values inspiring those responses, and commitment to what is decided as a policy of action are also needed.

While what is to be done in practice in each case must be decided in the light of the particular situation, what should be its final goal is clear. As Alex's mother once put it, the goal must be that each handicapped person – and indeed every person – be helped to live as full a life as is practicable. The resulting practical questions are important and frequently complex. They leave unanswered, however, the question of what constitutes the worth of a person, and in particular the worth of a severely handicapped person. If, as has been argued, the answer is not to be found in establishing the contributory worth of a person, and in the case of the severely handicapped particularly in the value of what she or he makes possible in the lives of others, how is the worth of a person to be established?

The notion of 'special education' is a reminder that handicapped people often require specialized assistance in tackling the problems of personal development and finding personal satisfaction. Some of them, however, present in their delight in simple things and their disinterest in achievement an example of peace in the world and with the world which provides an exemplary contrast to the ambition-driven and strife-ridden experiences of discontented life known by many people, and not least by many who are justifiably regarded as gifted and privileged. In this respect the smile of Alex in shaking hands stands in judgement on those who fail to be happy because they are so predominantly future-directed. He enjoyed the value of the present – and thus experienced the content which is perhaps an overlooked element in Jesus' call to his hearers to reflect on the birds and the flowers and to 'put away anxious thoughts' about the future (Matthew 6.25). In spite of the viciousness, corruption, pain and ugliness that is part of human experience every day, there is also good to be felt in what now is. That good is to be enjoyed.

Delight in the present and absence of concern about the future is not, of course, the whole pattern for life. According to the Matthean passage just cited, we are also to seek 'God's kingdom and justice' (Matthew 6.33). Nevertheless, there is a serious danger in stressing, for example with Pannenberg, future-orientated freedom as the dominant characteristic of human being and 'pure futurity' as the decisive characteristic of God. The result of such emphases is liable to be an activist conception of human being as a 'limit-transcending' existence which only participates in the divine as it endeavours to transform the present world through love (cf. Pannenberg 1971: 233, 249). When this happens, two mistakes are made. In the first place, fully human existence is considered to find its ideal in the creatively discontented, in those whose ideal is the God who is restlessly active. Doubts are thus cast on the authentic humanity of those, such as some of the severely handicapped, for whom it is inappropriate to speak of future-orientated activity. Such a view of the divine and the human, however, overlooks the image of God as one who, having seen that what had been made was good, ceased from work and blessed the day when the work that had to be done was complete (cf. Genesis 2.2f). This image is not the whole story of the divine and of the human, but it is part of it. In the second place, the values in present experiences are easily overlooked in a gnostic activism which is dominated by a negative view of the present world and by the pursuit of a future that contrasts radically with it. In these respects the ways in which some handicapped people find intense joy in what is given in the present moment bring to our attention a quality of human being which is too often ignored.

Nevertheless, while handicapped people have (sometimes enormous) needs that require special help, and while some of them at least provide a special challenge to a future-directed activist view of human existence, in one fundamental respect at least it is a mistake to regard such people as being special. As was pointed out earlier in this study, they are persons like everyone else. Each of them has his or her individual capacities and limitations, just as every other person has. There is consequently a danger in talking about handicapped people as 'the handicapped', as if their position in life is fundamentally different from that of other people. This is especially the case when the description is taken to imply that others have greater worth because, according to certain standpoints, they have superior and not merely different capacities.

What, however, is the worth of a person, however handicapped or however gifted? In the opening chapter I described how in a paper (Pailin 1988: 20ff) I took up Whitehead's description of God as 'the poet of the world'. According to this model God's saving activity is twofold. 'With tender patience' God stirs the creation by the divine vision of 'truth, beauty, and goodness', and God preserves 'each actuality in the temporal world' by incorporating it in the divine reality (Whitehead 1978: 346, 350). I now consider, however, that this exposition of Whitehead's insights is an indefensibly élitist view of salvation in so far as it implies that the worth of a person is established by her or his contributions to the divine reality. What is wrong with this élitism is not that it is contrary to a socialist mania for egalitarianism. (Such a socialist ideology might in turn be criticized on the grounds that it denies the worth of a particular individual as that individual by confusing equality with uniformity.) What is wrong with it is that it implies that there is little or no worth in the being of those who have little or no creative achievements to contribute to God's experience.

Underlying this understanding of the divine and the human is the contributory notion of worth. Earlier in this chapter I have argued that any attempt to establish the worth of severely handicapped people by claiming that they contribute to the fullness of the lives of other people is fundamentally flawed. Equally unsatisfactory is any attempt to establish that worth on the basis of contributions to the divine experience. It is derisible to think of a human being, however creative, making a significant impact upon the divine. The action of the captain of a stranded super-tanker who poured a cup of coffee over the side of the ship in order to decrease the weight of the ship and to increase the depth of the ocean would be thought ludicrous. So too would the action of a person who sent fivepence to the Treasury to reduce the National Debt. Is it any the less ludicrous to think that it is possible for a human being to add so significantly to the divine experience that thereby he or she is able to establish the worth of his or her being? Those who think that it is possible have forgotten that although to a large extent God must be conceived by human beings in the image of the human (cf. Pailin 1990: 31ff), the reality of God is not to be reduced to the level of the human. The perishing of creatures and the decay of what they produce are better symbols of the significance of their efforts than the notion that those efforts secure for them everlasting worth in the divine. In relation to the *scale* of the divine reality, the difference between the efforts of a Michelangelo and of an Alex are not important. No one establishes her or his particular worth in any significant way by what they contribute to the divine awareness of all events.

Furthermore, it is not because a person's contributions to the divine are so minuscule in relation to the boundlessness of the divine that this way of trying to establish the worth of a human being is basically unsatisfactory. As will shortly be discussed, the notion of contributory worth is itself intrinsically unsatisfactory in so far as it suggests that the worth of a human being is determined by the actions of that person as an agent. Although it is only possible to use this notion to establish the ultimate worth of human beings by maintaining that God receives all contributions, it basically puts forward an anthropocentric view of value. Ultimate worth, however, can only be established on a theocentric basis. While, therefore, there is much in the model of divine salvation suggested by Whitehead's remarks which I still affirm (cf. Pailin 1989: 208ff), Alex's gentle touch on me has brought me to see that on its own it is inadequate. If, however, divine salvation affirms the worth of all human beings, whatever their condition, whatever their capacities, and whatever they manage to achieve, how are this salvation and this worth to be understood?

What was said about the ludicrousness of regarding a cup of liquid as a significant contribution to the ocean or fivepence as a significant contribution to the National Debt may seem questionable in view of the way in which Jesus commended a 'poor widow' for her contribution to the Temple treasury. The important thing about her gift of 'two tiny coins' was, of course, not the difference which it made to the balance in the treasury, but what it meant for her. She had given 'all that she had to live on' (Mark 12.41ff). But why does her generosity matter if it made no difference to the treasury and if, had Jesus not chanced to look that way, it may well have contributed nothing to the experience of others in the community?

Does her action matter in the end because God appreciated it? If so, why is that important? Is God, for instance, to be thought of as valuing that widow because she gave, but not some other widow who kept her money? If the former acted as she did because she was generous, and the latter as she did because she was selfish, or if the former acted recklessly and the latter prudently, or if the former was seeking thereby to cadge favours from God whereas the latter was concerned about how to feed her children, would it have made any difference to the quality of God's concern for each of them? Of course God would know why each acted as she did and so would have a clear grasp of the moral value of what she did. It would be wrong, however, to go on to hold that, because some actions delight God more than others, God would have more concern for one who acted generously or prudently or thinking of her family, than for another who acted selfishly or recklessly or to cadge divine favours. The grace of God is not like that. It is for all, indiscriminately.

This does not imply that God does not give a damn about what a person does or does not do. How people think and act affects to an important degree the quality of their experiences of life. Those who make appropriate responses to love find delight, while those who make inappropriate ones find pain. Accordingly, such matters are of concern to all who love them, and especially, therefore, to God. On the other hand, what the parables of the lost sheep, the lost coin and the prodigal son (cf. Luke 15) suggest is that the divine love is not to be thought of as biased towards those who respond positively to it. If anything, the opposite is the case: 'It is not the healthy that need a doctor, but the sick' (Matthew 9.12; cf. 10.6ff; 15.24). As the anxiety of the shepherd, the housewife and the father is for the 'lost', so God's concern is for those whose quality of life is deprived because they fail to appreciate the divine love that constitutes the heart of reality. Whatever was the motive for the widow's gift, it is not relevant to establishing her importance to God and God's concern for her. What she did is important, rather, because it illustrates the total commitment that is an appropriate response to the divine. It would be pleasing to be able to add that it shows that she understood this and, even more pleasing, that she was making a total response because this is what her awareness of the love of God naturally evoked in her. Unfortunately neither claim is required by the evidence. We just do not know why she acted as she did!

Reflection on the widow's gift in relation to the gospel of the grace of God thus leads to the conclusion that whatever the significance of her action may be, it does not establish her fundamental worth. In a similar way, as has been mentioned, thought about Alex brought me to recognize that the fundamental worth of a person is not to be determined by his or her contributions, whether to other human beings or to the divine experience. Although every person (and maybe every actual entity) enjoys a certain degree of creative freedom to establish novel syntheses as moment by moment she or he responds to what comes to be in his or her environment, the worth of each person does not lie in the results of what she or he determines to be and to do. The contributory notion of value is a fundamentally mistaken way of seeking to establish the ultimate worth of any persons, even when the contribution is to the divine experience.

To hold this does not, of course, imply that handicapped people, even those who are very severely handicapped indeed, may not enrich the lives of others in important ways. Many

of those who share with those who are handicapped know
that the contrary can be the case. As Alex's mother puts it in
her description of his life, he 'seemed to have a special
magic'. Meeting him could be a gracefully enriching
experience. It is not, however, in such contributions – in his
'works' – that Alex's worth lies. And the same is true of
everyone else.

Where, then, does the real worth of persons fundamentally
lie? It is grounded not in what they can or do give, but in
what they can be given. Worth is not a quality that belongs
to a person in herself or himself; it is a matter of a
relationship with another person. It makes no difference
whether we think of an object like a painting or a book, a car
or a house, a lump of coal or a diamond on a ring, an old
jacket or new shoes, or whether we have in mind a person –
Alex or his father, you or me, any Tom, Dick or Harriet.
Worth is something that is bestowed by being loved, being
wanted, being respected, and being cherished. It is not a
quality that is inherent in an object or a person: it is a quality
that is given to an object or a person by another. Except for
the unique case of God (in whose reality what is regulative
for all others is instantiated – cf. Pailin 1990: 80ff), the
basis of worth is essentially other than what is held to be of
worth, even of fundamental worth.
   The point can easily be illustrated by thinking of the
values that are put on familiar objects. Sometimes supposed
experts – valuers, dealers, brokers – suggest that there is a
kind of objective standard by which the proper value of an
object can be determined. This is not so – although their
suggestion may help them to persuade us to buy or sell at
their figure! In the end the value that something has *for me*
depends on what it is worth to me. I am being conned if I am
persuaded to think differently. And the same applies to
everyone. When I indulge myself in buying an antiquarian
book, the critical questions are how much do I want it and
how much do others want it. The answer to the latter will
guide what the bookseller asks; the answer to the former will
decide what I am prepared to offer. It is the same whether
we think of the value of our labour or the price of a Picasso or
the price of shares in a company. Many complex factors may

influence how we consider the worth of an object (scarcity, desirability, likelihood of appreciation in value, amount of work in producing it, etc.), but in the end it is what it is worth to us that is determinative. Thirty-five years ago a bookseller where I was a student sold a pile of seventeenth and eighteenth century folio volumes in good condition for a shilling each (five pence for the younger reader), and still found difficulty in getting rid of them: now it would not be surprising to find a bookseller asking a thousand times that much for those volumes and getting it without too many problems. Fashions change, and values with them – as any manager of a fashion store knows only too well!

This understanding of value, however, does not only apply to the books and houses, cars and clothes that we may think of buying and selling, and whose value can thus be declared in terms of money. It also – and more interestingly for our purposes here – applies to things upon which a particular individual may place far greater value than others would. Consider, for instance, the threadbare teddy-bear that sits in a girl's bedroom. Granted that it has no antiquarian interest (for it is surprising what things turn out now to be valuable 'antiques'!), at a jumble sale it might well be hard to give it away, never mind to sell it. Its owner, however, might regard it as one of the most precious things which she has. If necessary she would give all her saved up pocket-money to ransom it from kidnappers! Or consider a lady dressed from the most expensive shops and wearing jewellery whose replacement costs would embarrass her insurers. She also wears a thin, plain ring whose gold-content is suspect. Because of what it means to her, however, that ring is for her the most precious thing on her.

Objects are sometimes said to be of 'sentimental value'. This phrase is normally understood to imply that what is so described has no 'real' value. 'Sentimental value' is taken to be an insignificant or even a bogus kind of value. To describe something as having 'only sentimental value' is thus to assert that the value which it has for a particular person is far greater than it 'really' has. This is a mistake. It may well be true that people in general do not treasure the object as greatly as does the person for whom it has 'sentimental value'. This does not mean, however, that the value which the object has for most people is its 'real' value while the value which it has for the person for whom it has 'sentimental value' is a less important, even an unreal or sham, kind of value. No object has any value (let alone any 'real' value, however that be determined) apart from its value for someone; and whatever value it has for someone is its value – for that person.

Worth, then, is not finally determined by reference to an impersonal register of 'market forces' or to 'a calculus of contributed satisfaction'. Allegedly objective ways of measuring worth in cash-value terms are particularly misleading. They disclose at best the secondary values, and often the shallow values, of a yuppy culture. Those who operate wholly by reference to them are performers in an impersonal society who, if they treat such tests as ultimate, show thereby that the depth of their souls has become silted up by materialistic concerns. By their behaviour they distort and betray the ultimate worth of everything, and particularly the ultimate worth of each and every person, as it is given by being the object of God's concern.

When the insight that value is fundamentally something which is given to rather than is inherent in an object is applied to the question of the worth of persons, and particularly to the question of the worth of severely handicapped persons, it follows that the fundamental worth of a person is to be seen to lie in the love of others for that person. Worth is not something that belongs to a person as a solitary individual. It is given to each person by the way that others, including – and ultimately – God, regard him or her.

What in that case is the worth of persons who justifiably consider that no one at all cares about them? A person who finds herself or himself in such a position is justified in feeling worthless. Furthermore, because no one at all cares about them, they may regard any affirmation of their own dignity as persons as practically impossible as well as pointless. Self-esteem is the product of being of worth to others. How, then, is it possible to claim that every person has worth? Think of a solitary old lady dying during the night on the pavement in a back street in Calcutta. No one knows her name. Next morning she will be removed like garbage. What worth can she be said to have? Or think of a boy who lives by his wits in São Paulo. He belongs to no family. Those who follow a contributory-value notion of worth should not object when a death-squad disposes of him in the darkness. It is one less troublesome parasite on the streets. Who can say that he has worth? To say that with education and opportunity he might make great contributions to society is to fall into the contributory notion of value and is a romantic way of evading the reality that no one cares whether he lives or not, let alone the reality that no one cares whether or not he receives education and opportunities.

If, then, the worth of a person is a matter of worth for someone else, and if no one cares for a certain person, does it follow that that person is worthless? The answer is, 'Yes in principle', and, for those who believe in God, 'No in practice.' In principle the conclusion follows from the premises. In practice, for those who have faith in the reality of God typical of the Judaeo-Christian-Muslim tradition (and probably of other traditions also that I am not competent to comment on), that conclusion does not state the truth about anyone. This is because its second premise is never true. There never is a person for whom no one at all cares if, as theistic faith holds, God, as the one whose relationships are always perfectly loving, knows each person each moment of her or his being.

There is a story of an old man who was found desperately ill and taken to a hospital. He was dirty and unkempt. He had no money. No one could discover who he was, who were his relations, or where he had come from. Two doctors examined him. Since it was a time when cultured people still could speak in Latin, and since they did not want the old man to understand their conclusions, they discussed his case in that language. Bearing everything in mind, it seemed to them that there was no point in wasting time and effort on his case. He was worthless and should be left to die. As they came to this conclusion, they heard the old man muttering. Bending over, they heard him ask in impeccable Latin, 'How can it be that one for whom God cares is of no worth?'

Worth, then, is something which is bestowed by the interest of others. Some people, however, may correctly perceive that there is no one in the human community who is much bothered about them, and in a few sad cases some may justifiably consider that no one at all has a positive attitude towards them. Should such people conclude that they have little or no worth? And what about other people? Does their worth vary with the interest that their fellow human beings have towards them? If worth is given by others, it may seem to follow that there is a scale of worth according to the interest that others show. Those who are much cared for by many have high worth on the scale; those for whom a few care a little come low on it. If this be the result of replacing a view of human worth based on a contributory norm of value with a given-by-others view, then the replacement may be less rather than more supportive of claims about the worth of human being. At least on the contributory view a person is not totally dependent upon the fickleness of circumstances and the attitudes of others.

What makes all the difference is the conviction at the heart of theistic faith that the reality of God has the character of all-inclusive love. All are loved. They are of ultimate worth because they are embraced within and cherished by the divine. What they experience as their being is not something that God merely observes from a distance: God shares their experiences of being as fully and as intimately as they do. (In more technical language, God is internally as well as externally related to every event.) No experience happens which God does not completely share. Each puff of existence, however minute, is lovingly noticed and incorporated within the everlastingly ongoing reality of God (cf. Pailin 1989: 76ff).

In the divine awareness, the distinctions between the paintings of a Mondrian and the splodges of an infant, between the profound comments of a theologian and Alex's blowing bubbles, between the skills of a neuro-surgeon and the clumsy movements of someone with cerebral palsy are not important so far as the worth of those persons is concerned. This does not mean that the distinctions are not important in terms of how these people may function – it would have been no good asking Alex to comment on this book (although some might treat his blowing bubbles as fair comment!). Nor would anyone expect a person whose movements are clumsy because of physical disabilities to be allowed to perform brain surgery on them. These functional differences between people (and also moral differences between them) must, however, be distinguished from their worth as individuals. Worth is a product of care by others.

Although the divine care for each individual does not vary according to the depth of the experiences of joy, effort, satisfaction and fun that attend each person's existence, it does not follow that the qualities of a person's experiences are of no account. God enjoys the wonder of a toddler watching a worm for the first time and the delighted amusement of the observing parents, the satisfaction of a researcher in solving a problem and the sense of achievement in a climber who has pioneered a new route, as intimately and as fully as the human beings having those experiences. These qualities all contribute to the richness of the wholly inclusive reality of the divine being. Nevertheless, it must be insisted, it is not anything that a person experiences or anything that a person produces that is the ground of her or his ultimate worth. Each person has ultimate worth just because he or she *is*, and as such is one whom God cherishes. On the other hand, just because there is no one and nothing which is not loved by God and so has no worth, it is justifiable to speak of each person and each object as having 'intrinsic' worth. Such a description, however, does not mean that worth is inherent in each person as a solitary existent; it belongs to each person because each is cherished by the divine and thereby given worth.

There is no need, then, for a person to be greedy for appreciation and hence restlessly to seek new experiences to contribute to the divine. Achievements are satisfying and not to be disparaged. In the end, however, a person's value is not determined by them. Just as children with good parents can relax in the basic confidence that they are loved by their parents whatever they do or do not succeed in doing, and just as pupils with good teachers know that they are respected whatever their abilities, so those who understand the reality of God discover that they are accepted for and as the persons that they are. And because they are valued by God as well as, it is to be hoped, by others, they are under no egocentric compulsion to be self-indulgent. Those who know that they are loved can love themselves and love others, not out of obedience to divine commands but because being loved evokes healthy love of self and love of others. As the

Johannine author put it, 'we love because he loved us first' (1 John 4.19).

Lest it be thought that the conclusion about the fundamental worth of human being which I have come to in thinking about Alex is eccentric, I close this chapter with two quotations. In *Radical Monotheism and Western Culture*, H. Richard Niebuhr writes that

> for radical monotheism the value-centre is . . . the principle of being itself . . . As faith, it is reliance on the source of all being for the significance of the self and of all that exists. It is the assurance that because I am, I am valued, and because you are, you are beloved . . . It is the confidence that whatever is, is good, because it exists as one thing among the many which all have their origin and their being, in the One – the principle of being which is also the principle of value. In Him we live and move and have our being not only as existent but as worthy of existence and worthy in existence. (Niebuhr 1961: 32)

A little later he puts it that those who regard 'Jesus Christ as the revelation of God' hold that 'the valuing, saving power in the world is the principle of being itself' and 'that the ultimate principle of being gives and maintains and re-establishes worth' (Niebuhr 1961: 43).

The other quotation is from the last page of Harry Williams' *The True Wilderness*. It begins with a quotation:

> In short, whoever you may be,
> To this conclusion you'll agree,
> When every one is somebodee,
> Then no one's anybody.

But those words of W. S. Gilbert are echoed in what the New Testament has to say about saints. They are not the spiritually aristocratic few, a sort of churchy House of Peers which appeals to the spiritual snob in each of us. All the members of Christ's Body are saints, and in the purpose of God Christ's Body includes all mankind . . . At All Saints Easter opens up like a fan to include everybody. (Williams 1965: 168)

Such is the 'good news' of salvation.

6

The 'good news' of salvation is
that we belong

Since, then, the worth of persons lies in the love of others for
them, and absolutely in the all-embracing love of God for
each individual, how is salvation to be understood and
expressed? What, in particular, is the gospel for those who
are handicapped, and how is it to be communicated to those
whose forms of handicap mean that their mental powers are
severely limited? These questions pose the issues to be
discussed in this chapter.

Before we consider how these questions may be answered,
however, two preliminary points should be noted. The first
is that what people understand is not limited to what they
can grasp and express conceptually. I once watched a young
man constructing a dry-stone wall. He was able with hardly
any hesitation to pick out a stone and lay it to produce what
seemed to me an amazingly solid and smooth-faced wall. We
got into conversation and it soon became apparent that at
school he would have been placed among the 'slow learners'.
I asked him how he decided which stone to put where. His
reply was interesting: 'I don't know. I'm not clever. But if I
don't pick the right stones, it'll look a mess and fall down.' So
far as walling was at issue, he was wrong about himself. He
did know and he was clever. When I tried to do it, I made an
unstable shambles! That he could not conceptualize his
knowledge in order to articulate what he knew was a different
matter. Also, in practice it was an unimportant matter.

Behind the young man's view of himself lies a widespread
prejudice, fostered by some unenlightened forms of education,
which leads people to regard explicit conceptual apprehension
as the paradigm form for all knowledge and understanding.
It is a mistaken prejudice.

As Polanyi's notion of the 'tacit dimension' reminds us

(Polanyi 1958; 1959; 1967), much of our understanding – including understanding which dominates our conscious judgements and guides our actions – is unformulated. It may be that some of it cannot be conceptually articulated. Among the reasons for this are that the knower is involved in the knowing, that the concepts available in any culture are limited, and, especially if theism be true, that some aspects of reality (including fundamental ones) are intrinsically beyond the bounds of human imagining. Nevertheless, while as Wittgenstein points out, 'What we cannot speak about we must pass over in silence,' it also needs to be appreciated, as he himself puts it, that certain things 'make themselves manifest' although they 'cannot be put into words' (Wittgenstein 1963: §§. 6.522; 7). Even for the most sophisticated persons, the bounds of what they may justifiably consider to be real may not be coterminous with the bounds of what their language allows them to express.

Sound reasoning, furthermore, is not confined to arguments whose premises and forms are explicit and precise, either actually or potentially. As Newman points out in relation to what he calls the illative sense (and as Locke (1690: IV, 17, 4) had seen earlier and Toulmin (cf. 1958: 188) was to rediscover later), in practice people often (indeed, generally) arrive at correct conclusions by processes of reasoning which are natural, informal and unconscious. Although skill in such reasoning may be, in Newman's terminology, 'departmental' in that one person may be notably proficient in reaching correct conclusions in one subject and another in a different one, and although education and experience generally enhance a person's proficiency in its exercise, the ability to perceive whether a story does or does not 'ring true' is not confined to those regarded as intellectually gifted (cf. Newman 1985: 219, 233).

Negatively this is seen in the way that many people, when presented with plausible arguments, can 'smell a rat' even though they not be able to identify where the case is faulty. Positively it is found in the way that many people are aware of what is the case even though they are unclear about why they perceive it to be so. A paediatric consultant, for example, told me that she finds it far more important to note that

parents 'feel' that something is 'wrong' with their child than
to rely on the evidence of symptoms which they offer to back
their judgement. Sometimes, of course, people make mistakes.
Juries may convict people of crimes which they did not
commit; instinctive assessments sometimes turn out to have
been disastrously mistaken; rogues manage to dupe even the
suspicious. Nevertheless, in spite of the imperfections of
human understanding, there are good grounds for trusting
the natural ability of 'common sense' and being suspicious of
logically sophisticated reasoning.

However, people differ in their capacity to understand and
to reason. To recognize that understanding is not limited to
what can be conceptually expressed and that sound reasoning
is not limited to what can be laid out in explicit structures
does not imply that all persons are equally competent in
what they can implicitly understand and unconsciously
reason about. Experience shows otherwise. People differ
both 'departmentally' (to use Newman's term) and in overall
competence. Mary quickly recognizes what a sick person
needs but she fumbles with engines; John 'has a way' with
engines but is not to be followed in his 'instinctive feel' for
the route on a trackless moorland. Alex's father has a breadth
of understanding whose depth Alex would probably have
never been able to equal on any matter even if he had lived to
old age. Whatever egalitarian ideals may and should inspire
educational policies and practice, the brute fact is that people
are not equal in their potentialities and, *a fortiori*, in their
attainments.

Consequently, it would be irresponsible to allow those
who are severely mentally handicapped to sit on juries or to
invest pension funds. They would not be able to appreciate
what is happening and what they should do. Some such
people are puzzled by the ordinary situations in which they
find themselves. Because they have to trust others to guide
them in what to do, they are particularly vulnerable to
deception and persuasion. It is wrong, however, to think that
for them education is wholly a matter of training in social
skills so that they can take part without risk and embarrass-
ment in communal life. The pattern of enquiry, experiment,
investigation, understanding and practice of enlightened (if

sometimes impracticable) educational practice applies to them as to all others but, and this is an important 'but', it has to be pursued in ways that are appropriate to them.

While, however, some people are extremely limited in their intellectual grasp of many things, it does not follow that they are without awareness and understanding. That they are unable to formulate intellectual judgements about love, care and the dignity of the person does not mean that they do not understand what it is to be loved, cared for and respected as a person – and, contrariwise, what it is to be ignored, neglected and denied dignity. Furthermore, because some people may not be able to follow talk about hypocrisy, it does not follow that they cannot appreciate the difference between those who make a superficial pretence of being concerned about them and others who show in relationships with them the warmth and patience of authentic fellowship. At the level of reality where it matters – that is, at the level of actual personal relationships – they may grasp (even if that grasp is tacit or implicit) a great deal about the nature of their relationships with other people and of what it means about their own worth as persons. So far, then, as to 'understand' is to be aware of and to make sense of what is the case, it is a mistake to confine it to what can be perceived, reasoned about and expressed explicitly in conceptual forms.

The second preliminary point that needs to be made before we consider the central issues for this chapter concerns the character of religious faith. The heart of living religious faith is not simply nor even primarily an intellectual assent to ideas which are grasped conceptually. Such assent is at best a secondary and partial perception of the content of faith. Even less is religious faith to be identified with the affirmation of credal formulae, or with consent to the conclusions of rational arguments, or with the performance of certain rites, or with the observation of certain moral principles. Authentic religious faith is a matter of an existential commitment to the reality of the divine which determines the basic character of a person's life. Where, as in theistic faith, the divine is understood to be a personal reality, faith refers to the manner in which individuals are aware of themselves as decisively related to that reality and seek to live out that relationship in appropriate ways.

For those who believe in God, faith is thus far more like a deep friendship than like being able to grasp Pythagoras' theorem. To have grasped the latter may have no more significance for how I live than many other things that I have been told – such as that absolute zero is minus 273 degrees Centigrade, that Alexander the Great crossed the now ruined bridge at Ani, that Jesus had a brother called James, and that (according to Cruden) there are 3,566,480 letters in the words in the Bible. Such items of information are, as Cruden remarks of the last one, 'more curious than useful'! If I forget any of them or discover that any of them is wrong, it is unlikely to make any difference to the character of my life.

Authentic religious faith is, in contrast, an understanding of the ultimate character of reality and an accompanying comprehensive attitude to which a believer is ultimately committed and by which the character of his or her life is basically formed. When accurately apprehended, it identifies what that person holds to be fundamentally the case in reality and the values and principles which she or he accordingly perceives to be decisive. It refers, in other words, to what finally makes an individual 'tick' as that particular person. The word 'God', as naming the object of theistic faith, refers to that which (or, rather, the one who) embodies this ultimacy in being and value. (It may be noted in passing that critics who object to such a claim on the grounds that it commits the 'naturalistic fallacy' – that is, the fallacy of attempting to derive what ought to be from what is – because of the way in which it links values with what is the case have failed to appreciate the peculiar nature of the reality of God [cf. Pailin 1990: 72].)

God is accordingly worshipped as the self-grounded ground of all whose nature determines the ultimate character and significance of whatever is. Not only is the existence of each non-divine entity held to be contingent upon the reality of God but also, as was maintained in the previous chapter, its worth is held to be finally and decisively determined by its worth for God. In principle, then, theists live as they do because they hold that what they consider to be the nature of

God determines the character of the fundamental structure and final worth of being in general and of their individual being in particular. In practice Christians (i.e., theists whose understanding of the material character of God is moulded by reference to Jesus as the Christ) are those who live in a way that is graciously open to the future because of their conviction that reality is grounded in the Holy One who is unconditionally ultimate, secure, reliable, caring and accepting.

'Salvation', according to this understanding of faith, connotes the existential state of being which is enjoyed by persons who may be described (cf. Ogden 1967: 47) in intellectual terms as having confidence in the ultimate worth or 'significance' of their lives in this world (whether or not they perceive that this confidence is only finally justified because they are of worth and significance to God) and who, by acting according to this faith, live in harmony with the basic character of reality as embodied in the divine. This positive interpretation of 'salvation' contrasts with common usage. For the latter the predominant characteristic of 'salvation' is that of 'deliverance from'. The description 'saviour' is hence applied to whoever makes it possible for us to escape from something undesirable (whether it be dying of exposure on a mountainside, or having to read a tedious thesis, or facing the just consequences of our wrong-doing, or being victims of the wrath of God). As a result remarks about salvation tend to have a predominantly negative emphasis. The stress is on what is avoided rather than on what is positively achieved. This is a pity. What is most important about salvation is not that some real or imaginary evil has been avoided (cf. Pailin 1991), but, where the evil is real and unavoidable (as with prisoners in a death camp or individuals facing terminal illness), that it has been transcended and, so far as is possible, that a richly satisfying quality of life has become actual. It is the latter, positive understanding of the notion of salvation which accords with John's report of Jesus' intention, namely, that he had 'come' so that people 'may have life, and may have it in all its fullness' (John 10.10).

This was the witness of the earliest Christians. They announced the salvation that comes with the recognition that 'nothing in all creation can separate us from the love of God'

(Romans 8.39). Knowing this as a reality, although conceptually 'it is beyond knowledge', empowers people to 'attain to fullness of being' which is the fullness of God's own being (Ephesians 2.18ff). Such a positive understanding of faith in God and of salvation lies behind Bonhoeffer's condemnation of the perverted evangelism which attempts to persuade people that, whether they be conscious of it or not, they are 'deeply involved' in 'problems, needs, and conflicts'. Thus they are told that their apparent 'happiness is really an evil, [their] health a sickness, and [their] vigour despair'. Such an attitude is, in Bonhoeffer's judgement, contrary to that of Jesus. He never questioned a person's 'health, vigour, or happiness'. Otherwise the records of his actions would not make sense: 'why should he heal the sick and restore strength to the weak?' (Bonhoeffer 1971: 341f; cf. 327ff). To believe the Christian gospel is to affirm the reality of God as the gracious ground of being whose presence is found in, whose will desires, and whose spirit promotes life, health, vigour and activity (cf. Bonhoeffer 1971: 312). It is to participate in the fullness of life enjoyed by those whose existence is characterized by the wholeness, sense of worth and creative openness which comes from being grounded in the faith that the ultimate reality is perfect love.

As Newman emphasizes with his distinction between the 'notional' and the 'real' (cf. Newman 1985: 12ff; Pailin 1969: 109ff), the 'knowledge' which is at the heart of this faith is not a merely intellectual recognition of the reality of the divine. It is neither like a precise idea of something that is wholly abstract nor like a notion which we might entertain about something we have been told about but have only grasped as a more or less vague thought. The 'knowledge' that a living faith rests on is an awareness of what we sense to be concretely the case. Even if we have no direct acquaintance with its object and only come to be aware of it by means of empathy and imagination, faith is primarily a conviction grounded in what is grasped as an actual reality.

Having outlined what is meant by understanding and by faith and salvation, we may turn to the central question for this chapter. How is the gospel of the Christian faith in God to be understood and expressed so that it may be grasped by those who are handicapped, in particular by those who are severely handicapped mentally? How, that is, may they be helped to know for themselves the 'saving' reality of the divine?

The basis for an answer to this question is not found by concentrating on the condition of handicapped people as if this made them a separate case. Although some people are so mentally limited that their conceptual grasp of the contents of their faith may be negligible, being so limited does not significantly affect how they may come to have an authentic faith in the reality of God. Just as the question of the worth of a handicapped person turns out to be the question of the worth of all human beings, so the way by which a handicapped person may come to be convinced of the saving reality of the divine is found on examination to be basically no different from that appropriate to human beings generally. How, then, do people come to authentic faith in God?

The life-promoting reality of God is not given to us to be inspected like a watch, tasted like a chocolate, or encountered like a friend. By what means, then, do we become aware of the divine?

Somewhat sadly I have to admit that only an odd person (perhaps one might also say a very odd person) is likely to arrive at a real apprehension of the reality of God through reading works of theology, whether they be learned tomes or popularizing interpretations of them (although this does not stop some of us writing them!). Books communicate ideas, but for most people (and perhaps for all) the information which is gained solely from books is restricted to the level of ideas entertained in the mind. Something more than reading is needed to bridge the gap from a grasp of ideas to a living awareness of the reality of the divine.

What is true of theological studies applies to religious writings in general, including those books which are regarded as 'sacred scripture'. According to their traditional self-understandings, Judaism affirms the Torah, Islam the Qur'ān, Buddhism the teaching of Gautama, and Christianity the Bible – and particularly its witness to the life and teaching of Jesus – as the normative source of insight into the divine. Those who do not stand within a particular tradition of faith, however, are not likely to find that simply reading its 'sacred scripture' by itself produces a living awareness of the reality of the divine. We become aware of this when we read the sacred texts of a faith other than our own. The materials may be interesting; they may contribute to our understanding of our own faith. Nevertheless, on their own they stay as materials which at best provoke reflection and at worst profound puzzlement as to why some people find them so important. Something more is needed to arouse a living faith in the reality of the divine.

For many people the spoken word is more impressive than the written – and the living word more convincing than the recorded. The presence of the speaker adds to the words a personal force which is not possible with written or recorded testimony. In spite of this, however, the amount of energy that preachers expend each week is hugely cost-ineffective. This is not because what preachers assert is untrue (although listening carefully to sermons may lead to the disturbing conclusion that some preachers are unable to distinguish between their fantasies and what is actually the case – but then this is typical of many propagandists). Nor is it simply a matter of the unfamiliar language that some preachers use. Most people are quickly able to pick up jargon when they find it significant. Preaching and other wholly verbal methods of communicating faith fail because what is stated, whether written or spoken, whether in sacred writings or uttered by stirring orators, is largely incapable of persuading us for long that reality is other than how we find it to be in our experience (or, to be more accurate, in our interpretation of our experiences of it). In spite of the relativity of our understanding of reality, there is a stubborn givenness about what is the case which undermines the claims of those who maintain that we create the reality in which we find ourselves through the language which we use to understand it. Fascinating and influential as words may be, they are media for communicating, shaping and grasping an awareness of what is the case; they do not constitute reality itself – as we confirm when we use such phrases as 'But you are only *saying* that' and 'But that is only is how *you* see it'.

The critical factor in bringing people to apprehend faith is its relationship to their experiences. Faith can only become real for people when it connects with their experiences and is recognized to make sense in terms of how life actually is for them. As a result the important, indeed often the decisive, media for awareness of the divine are encounters with other people.

This does not mean that experiences of the non-personal aspects of reality do not significantly affect the formation of a person's faith. Those to whom the natural world appears to be predominantly orderly and reliable are often unaware how much they take its characteristics for granted. It is when something happens to undermine their confidence in it that they show how much its assumed character has moulded them. This may be seen, for example, in people who have unexpectedly experienced an earthquake or a severe illness: finding that they can no longer rely on the 'solid earth' or on their bodies, they feel insecure. They have to come to terms with a different (and a more realistic) appreciation of the character of the natural world of which they are contingent, finite and mortal constituents.

The major influence upon the formation of a person's faith, however, is the character of that individual's relationships with other people, and especially with close friends. From birth the way in which people develop is profoundly affected by how they are treated by and encouraged to respond to those around them. Negatively this means that there is a great deal of difference between an individual learning that 'sanguine' means 'hopeful' rather than 'resigned' (a discovery which came embarrassingly late in my education!) and that person finding that someone who has been trusted as a friend has persistently abused that trust. The latter discovery not only hurts the particular relationship: it may deeply disturb the person's relationships with others by undermining his or her confidence in the trustworthiness of people generally. Positively this is seen in the way that individuals grow in self-esteem and confidence as they find that others are concerned about them and respect them as the persons that they have come (and continue to come) to be.

Furthermore, those who experience grace in their encounters with others, who know themselves to be loved, who find themselves in a caring community and who are aware that others respect them as individuals that are of worth, are the ones who are most likely to begin to sense that what they find in such experiences is a symbol* of the gracious love that constitutes the ground of all being – that is, in theistic language, that characterizes the nature of God. Not only is it the case, as the first letter of John maintains, that a person who does not love those 'whom he has seen' cannot love 'God whom he has not seen' (1 John 4.19f), it is also the case that persons who have no sense of being loved by other people around them are unable to become aware of the love of God for them. In practice, therefore, the means by which people become aware of what they consider to be the ultimate nature of reality is rather humdrum. God is primarily found through the impact of day-to-day encounters with others, not through the exalted mysteries of ecstatic experiences. The incarnation is a continuing reality.

The importance of words in these matters, whether read or heard, is not that they create a new state of reality but that they help people to become conscious of the nature of their situation. In the case of religious faith, words provide a way by which people may become aware that what they experience in some of their encounters with other people is an experience, however limited and distorted, of the character of their relationship to God, the ultimate and all-embracing reality whose concern is the ground of the fundamental value of each individual.

It is important, however, to note two points in this respect. The first is that what is important about the relationship with God which faith names is its reality and not the perception of its reality. It is like being healthy: self-conscious awareness that I am healthy is secondary and usually is trivial in comparison to being healthy. The actuality is what matters, not our self-conscious identification of it. Similarly what matters, to God and for human beings, is that people's lives are determined by the reality of God's love, not that they can consciously identify God as the origin of that love – although it should also be noted that those who do identify it

---

*'Symbol' is here meant in the strong form employed by Paul Tillich when he states that a 'symbol participates in the reality of that for which it stands' (Tillich 1951: 265). As such the notion of symbol resembles that of a sacrament as an earthly instantiation (and more than a mere expression) of the divine–human relationship.

correctly are the more likely to be able to respond effectively to it.

The second point is that most people have very different kinds of experience. Experiences of being loved are mingled with experiences of being rejected, of being treated as having worth with being treated with contempt, of being affirmed with being ridiculed, of being welcomed with being ignored, and of being respected with being despised. If, therefore, the faith which is engendered by a person's experience is to be coherent, it cannot simply be the product of that person's unsifted encounters. A principle of selection must be involved by which the individual, almost certainly unconsciously, comes to regard only certain kinds of experience as authentic symbols of the ultimate character of reality – for theistic faith, as symbols of God. What, however, determines the principle of selection?

Culture, mediated informally through the different circles of a person's social environment much more than through formal teaching, has a major influence on each individual's principle of selection. It is hard for a person to resist the pressures of social conformity to share the prevailing attitudes. Nevertheless, individuals are not condemned to be wholly social constructions. A major factor in preventing this is that the social environment itself is not uniform. A choice, albeit a choice which again is largely, if not completely, unconscious, has to be made between competing and conflicting patterns of faith.

There are doubtless many factors which influence that choice. In most cases, however, two factors dominate. One is the individual's basic desire for affirmation as a person; the other is the need for congruence with what the individual senses to be the inescapable character of reality. The former may be satisfied in a way that is individualistic (affirming each person primarily as an independent entity) or corporate (affirming each person's significance in terms of being part of a whole) or by some balance of the two. In one way or other, however, the person is affirmed as having worth. Whether it expresses the survival of an evolutionary powerful instinct for self-preservation or conforms to the basic existential character of human being, this factor ensures that people respond to what offers to establish the worth of their being who they are. The other factor is the individual's perception of the basic character of reality. This factor inescapably begs the question to some extent, for what is perceived to be the character of reality is affected by the principles of interpretation which mould the apprehension of experiences of it. Nevertheless, the circularity is not wholly vicious. As has been mentioned already, there is a stubborness about what we experience to be the case so that it at least refuses to fit some interpretations that are placed upon it even if it does not compel us to adopt only one way of understanding it.

How, then, is faith in God to be communicated? Primarily it is by nurturing people through personal relationships in which they are both affirmed as persons and find a realistic way of believing that the ultimate nature of reality is one of gracious, sustaining love. The affirmative character of faith is not enough. It is equally important that it be experienced as a realistic understanding of the ultimate nature of reality. Its credibility as a way of dealing with reality as they find it is what warrants people, having used their reason to reflect critically on what is offered to them, in wholeheartedly committing themselves to faith in God as true rather than regarding it as attractive but fictional wishful thinking.

In terms of the Christian faith this way of understanding how faith is communicated means that the congregations constituting the empirical church should see themselves as willed by God to be, as Bonhoeffer puts it, 'the means whereby he makes use of the social connection between men to spread his rule over men' (Bonhoeffer 1963: 159). The church should realize that now 'the church is the presence of Christ, as Christ is the presence of God'. It does not, however, follow from this (*pace* Bonhoeffer's contrary suggestion in this early work) that congregations should hold that today Christ is '*only* present in the church' (Bonhoeffer 1963: 101; my italics). The presence of God is not so confined.

It might seem that the case of those who are handicapped has largely been ignored in the preceding discussion of the nature of saving faith. Such a judgement would be mistaken. Not only is salvation, as the state of existence enjoyed by those who have confidence in the ultimate worth of their lives, the same for all persons, however handicapped or however richly gifted. The way to it is also basically the same. It is through being loved by other people (and this includes being told that they are loved in words as well as in deeds) that individuals come to grasp the all-embracing reality of God's love for them.

Some people have an inner compulsion to be sure of the credibility of their sense of belonging to God. As Anselm recognized, there is within faith an intrinsic urge for self-understanding – *fides quaerens intellectum* (faith seeking understanding). To a large extent this is healthy. For those who have the intellectual capacity, theological reflection on the contents and justification of their faith is a proper way of seeking to ensure that their faith is correctly understood, applied and given assent.

In the case of some people, however, the demands of the intellect are so strong that they hinder the ability to live by faith in the gracious goodness of God. The need to convince themselves of the rational justification of their self-understanding makes it hard for them to accept the reality of what faith presents. Either because, like children crying for the moon, they want a certainty that is not possible or because, like an insecure authoritarian, they cannot face the possibility of being found to be wrong, they are unable to commit themselves. Like dithering would-be lovers, they spend their life in unhappy hesitation. Others do commit themselves as best they can but, having faith, suffer from a constant urge to inspect it. The result is that their faith is unable to develop effectively. Like a plant that is frequently pulled out of the ground to inspect how its roots are growing, it never has a chance to mature.

Nevertheless, whether a person's rational reflections upon faith are appropriate or excessive, the results are *about* faith. They are not what faith itself *is*. Where it is consciously apprehended, the saving faith proclaimed in the Christian gospel is that state of being in which the individual is aware of being grounded upon and embraced within the divine love and lives accordingly. For many people, however, the reality of this faith is a mode of existence in which and by which they live without being explicitly conscious of it. As babies are embraced by parental love long before they can be intellectually self-conscious of their situation, so the love of God gives worth to all. It is not confined to those who know *about* it.

What, then, of handicapped persons? How is saving faith to be presented and known by those whose understanding is unimpressed with or cannot cope with abstract notions? The answer lies in the practice of that faith. Through the examples of the lives of others around them, and especially through the behaviour of others towards them, handicapped persons may find for themselves the reality of existence that is grounded in confidence in the grace of God and hence is radically open both to others in love and to the future in hope. Of course, the ways in which that confidence, openness, love and hope may be actualized will vary with the individual. What is important is not how they are actualized but that they are actualized appropriately and as fully as possible for each individual.

But, it may still be asked, how is this to be achieved? How may handicapped people come to know for themselves the grace of God? It is the same way that anyone, from infancy to decrepitude, comes to know it. It is by smiles and handshakes and hugs, by interest in the individual as that particular person, by patience and sharing, by taking that person's feelings and wishes seriously, and by being concerned that that person should contribute to the experience of the community. In other words it is by actions that make the individual aware that she or he is important – has worth – because he or she is important to others. It is by loving that person.

What is involved is not mere acceptance as part of the community, the bare acknowledgement of a right to be present. Acceptance can be so cold that it freezes to death a person's capacity for saving faith. Nor is what is involved the opposite of this – a concern that smothers others with an outpouring of supposedly loving interventions that critically fail to respect them as persons. Some attempts to express love stifle the other in satisfying the ego-trip of the lover. What is needed, rather, is that interested cherishing that balances concern with respect for the dignity of the other, that makes help available while leaving space for the other to be (so far as is possible) genuinely autonomous, that loves without expecting to be loved, and that does not impose itself but waits to be asked – and having been asked does not take advantage of the opening. This is the love that nurtures.

Nevertheless, the questioner may persist, this describes personal relations in the human community: how are handicapped people to come to know the grace of *God*? The answer is what has been said. The idea of God may not make a lot of sense to some people, and for some it may make no sense at all, but the reality of loving care, reverence and respect from others can be known for it can be experienced. Such experience, furthermore, may lead those who enjoy it to a sense of their fundamental worth and a trusting confidence in the gracious goodness of what ultimately is the case. In this way their awareness of being loved by others in the human community acts as a living symbol through which they become aware in practice of the reality of God even if they never consciously identify it.

The incarnation of the divine is thereby experienced as a present, continuing reality: what Christians believe to have been normatively disclosed in Jesus as the Christ is revealed to people today – and especially to those whose handicap makes them unable to grasp the content of abstract notions – through those around them. The divine–human relationship perceived through Jesus is a relationship which is real now, whenever and wherever the 'now' of the present moment may be, in and through acts of human love. As Evelyn Underhill puts it, 'I come in the little things, Saith the Lord' so as to 'Pass the low lintel of the human heart' (Underhill 1917: 524–5).

But, the questioner may still persist, do handicapped people recognize the divine referent of the symbol? Are they aware that it is *God* who is the all-embracing love that assures them of their fundamental worth and inspires in them a trusting confidence in the gracious goodness of what is ultimately the case? To that question the best reply is another question: Does it matter? Is God so self-seeking that God wants recognition? Such a desire projects on the divine our self-centredness and insecurity. It is not an aspect of love. Love loves. It does not seek payment.

In some respects the gifts at Christmas which may best express the grace of God for humankind are those which appear in children's stockings anonymously or with the label 'From Father Christmas'. In contrast to the view which holds that 'gifts' are only complete when they are received with gratitude to the donors, these gifts are to be enjoyed for their own sake and without the burden of appropriate response. There is no one to whom the children have to be grateful. They do not even have to pretend to be delighted with the gift if they are not! There are no donor's wishes to be respected and no social bonds of reciprocity implied. These gifts are given purely to give delight and not to develop relationships, not even to develop 'bonds of love' between persons. They are pure gifts. If any ulterior motive may be used to justify them, it is that of arousing in the recipients a sense of the mysterious graciousness that is the ground of all being. So, too, is the divine love. It does not matter whether or not its source is correctly perceived. It is trivial what names it goes under (except in so far as correctly identifying it enhances a person's ability to respond to it). What is important is that it be known as a reality. If, then, the experiences of handicapped people develop into a trusting confidence that they exist in a universal reality that is fundamentally loving (and so profoundly accepting, cherishing and caring), the Christian gospel has been preached to them experientially and effectively. Nothing more is necessary.

So far as the worshipping life of the Church is concerned, the sacraments of baptism and the eucharist are ways in which the reality of God's love is expressed. It is important that handicapped people share in them.

In recent decades there has been a growing failure to recognize the evangelical significance of the sacrament of baptism. There has been pressure to restrict baptism to the children of practising believers or, even worse, to restrict it to those able to make sincerely and with understanding a profession of Christian faith. This is to give the impression that the divine–human relationship is conditional upon human achievement as well as upon divine grace. Pushed to the extreme of permitting baptism only for professing believers and regarding it almost as a condition of salvation (and certainly as a condition of proper membership of the community of those who have saving faith), it threatens to promote a return to the false doctrine of salvation by works, even if they are works of the understanding (i.e., of 'correct belief') and not the more socially useful works of charity.

Such views satisfy the desire among some believers to feel that they are special as well as different. Belonging to the club is a privilege. Something is needed – an entrance fee – before a person is worthy to join. If nothing more is to be demanded, at least entrants must show that they accept the rules of the club.

What is presented when the sacrament of baptism is administered to a baby is the opposite of such an attitude. Saving faith is not a matter of belonging to a club called the church and baptism is not satisfying an entrance requirement. Neither does God play a game of pretending that the baby is professing faith through the parents (and/or godparents). God knows, as we do if we are realistic, that the baby has no idea about what is going on. Like being cuddled and changed, fed and burped, injected and cooed at, a baby experiences baptism as another of those things that happen and of which in later life she or he will have no recollection. If the parents, family, friends, minister and congregation are honest, they may well prefer the baby to be asleep and so unaware of what is happening. Baptism is less noisy in that case! It does not matter. The focus of attention should not be on the baby and even less on the parents, the minister or the church. It should be on God, for it is the unconditional character of God's care for every person – and so for this baby – that the sacrament re-presents.

Baptism, that is, is a sacrament of God's grace. In the case of a baby it affirms that this person, like all other persons, is accepted, embraced and loved by God. This is not because of what this person has done or believed, nor because of what others have done and believed on this person's behalf. It is just because God's grace excludes none. Belonging to the family of God is like belonging to natural families. It occurs simply through the fact of being born.

Those, therefore, who try to limit baptism to believers or to the children of believers (and who presume to judge who satisfy that condition) arrogate to themselves a power of discrimination which God rejects. There are no boundaries to the family embraced by God. Remember Alex. When he was baptized he was surrounded by people who were concerned about him and who recognized him as a part of their community, whether of family, or of friends, or of the church. They acknowledged their responsibilities for his welfare. The crucial thing that happened, however, was that they were reminded of what had always been and would always be the case for Alex (as for every other person), namely, that God loved him without reservation. He was totally and unconditionally embraced by God.

And what was true for Alex has been and is and will be true for any person just because that person exists. Rather than limit baptism, therefore, to those who meet certain conditions, in some respects the church would better affirm the unconditional love of God for all expressed in this sacrament if it used a fire-hose to sprinkle everyone indiscriminately as they passed by – although the theological justification of such behaviour might surprise the police and worry the magistrates! In one respect, however, such undifferentiating behaviour would be grossly mistaken. This is because the love of God is utterly discriminating, not because it is restricted to only some people but because it applies to each person as that particular person. That is why naming the person being baptized is an important part of the sacrament of baptism: it symbolizes that God cares for *this* person (as for every other person) individually. The divine love does not pour out like sunshine which warms whoever happens to stand in the sun's rays but of whom the sun is unaware. God's love of all persons is actualized as an individual relationship with each person.

It does not matter that some handicapped people may never make any sense of the sacrament of baptism. What does matter is that what the sacrament proclaims about God is seen to apply to each handicapped person – and to every other person. God knows each of them by name and loves them. Baptism also reminds the congregation that those who profess to love God must do the same – or be judged to be liars (cf. 1 John 4.20f).

When attention turns from the sacrament of baptism to that of the eucharist, questions may arise about the participation of handicapped people. Should they be allowed to communicate when they have little or no understanding of the theological significance of what they are doing?

One answer to this question would be to point out that if only those who satisfy tests of correct understanding are to be allowed to communicate, the number of communicants will decline dramatically – and there will be arguments about whether those who are held to be qualified have provided the 'correct' answers! The way to the Lord's table would be littered with theological disputes – and disputes which might turn into such arcane niceties that one would wonder if God enjoyed brain-teasers.

A more fruitful approach to the issue is to consider the practical question of *when* children should be allowed to share in the bread and wine at the eucharist. Some people suggest that they should wait until they are old enough to make an intelligent, rational commitment and, in certain ecclesiastical traditions, have had that commitment endorsed in a service of confirmation. This answer, however, verges on being a version of the demand that they satisfy some test of correct understanding. To make a significant profession of faith demands a level of mature reflection and self-understanding that small children do not have – and which some handicapped people may never have. Who, in any case, is to decide when a person's response has become satisfactory?

Others suggest that children ought not to communicate until they are old enough to behave in a seemly manner at the eucharist. Never mind what they may think is happening, at least let us have dignity! Babies may scream at their baptism, but those who cannot 'behave properly' should not be allowed to upset the solemn time when the congregation eats the consecrated bread and drinks the consecrated wine. I confess that I like order, and when the question arose of children's participation at the church which I attend, this was the response that attracted me. I now consider that it is the wrong response for at least three reasons.

One reason why it is the wrong response is that it fails to appreciate that the eucharist is a token meal of God's family in which the bread and wine symbolically re-present the reality of God's saving love for all – and which, according to some traditions, is also to be seen as a foretaste of the eschatological feast. At heart it is not a sacred mystery to be reserved for the initiated. Saving faith is not a matter of secret and obscure gnosis. It is an all-embracing love which is celebrated in a family meal. A useful model for understanding it is a family party.

While parents may sometimes prefer to feed their children first so that they can enjoy a quiet meal later, in a family which cares for its members such separation is unacceptable when it comes to celebrations. Then everyone must take part – even if the toddlers yank the table-cloth, spill drink, drop food on the carpet and demand attention at most inconvenient moments. When the family celebrates, all the members who can should take part – from the dribbling old man who is too confused to grasp what it is all about to the new-born baby who is asleep. Should not the family of God gathered at the eucharist similarly exclude none?

A second reason why my initial response was wrong is that this response fails to recognize who is responsible for sending out the invitations to the meal. The host is not the minister or the church leaders or even the congregation as a whole. The host is God, and the invitation is an expression of divine grace. People are accepted at the eucharist not because of what they believe or do or are but because, and simply because, God invites them. Those who limit access in effect presume to know better than God who is acceptable. They need to correct their views.

Some years ago I was asked by a vicar to help him with the midnight Holy Communion at Christmas. Being a sheltered Methodist working in a university, I had no idea what went on in a town-centre church as the pubs emptied on Christmas Eve. In the congregation there were some swaying figures singing the carols with more *bonhomie* than reverence – and other sober church members who looked pained. I asked the vicar what we were to do if the former came to share the bread and wine. He laughed – 'Give it them. Who are we to judge who is worthy? What do you think Christmas is about?' It may be hard to accept, but it is not the job of the church to decide whom God should entertain.

The third reason why access to the eucharist should not be limited to those who believe is that it is, in John Wesley's words, a 'converting ordinance'. While Wesley may be wrong in describing the apostles gathered at the Last Supper as 'unconverted' (on the grounds that they were not yet believers who had 'received the Holy Ghost'), he correctly expresses the mind of Christ in suggesting that the elements are a means of grace which should be given to the unconverted to convert them as well as to the converted to confirm them (cf. Wesley 1819: 42; 1820: 224f). Sharing in the eucharist is not just a way in which Christians are presented with symbols to reinforce their awareness of the basis of their saving faith. It is also a way in which others may come to discover it.

When, therefore, I consider the place of children in the eucharist in terms of what that service expresses, and not in terms of my dislike of 'conduct prejudicial to good order and discipline', I realize that it is right for them to partake. They are part of the family of God. It is important that the central service of the church should recognize it. The same argument applies to the situation of those who are handicapped. It does not matter that the behaviour of some of them may be awkward, nor even that it is disruptive: they are part of the family. The church fails to be the family of God when holiness is confused with orderliness. It did not matter when Alex wheezed in the worship: with his hole in the heart breathing was sometimes difficult. The important thing was that he shared in the worship and was loved.

Nor does it matter if handicapped people do not grasp the basic theological significance of the eucharist, let alone some of the niceties of doctrines about transubstantiation, consubstantiation and commemoration. There are not many in any congregation who do! Theological competence is not a prerequisite of saving faith. For that we may be thankful. The heart of the eucharist is not found in conceptual awareness but in practice, in sharing a ritual act. In sharing in it as one of the family, perhaps simply at the level of being included rather than excluded, some who are handicapped may be helped to discern experientially the reality of God's love for them. When this happens, the service symbolizing the Christian understanding of God fulfils its role in Christian worship.

The offering (by God to us) and receiving (by us from God) of bread and wine symbolizes the divine–human relationship. So far as the links between the family of God on earth are concerned, the act of giving and receiving the 'kiss of peace' in worship should be recognized to be another important symbolic activity. It is not just an excuse to give someone an embarrassed handshake or even a peck on the cheek. It is an activity in which those present recognize that they are part of one family. If the result is that the service gets a bit disorganized at that point, so be it. The pattern for it is not the line of officials to greet a visiting dignitary but the happy mixing of a family being reunited at an airport. In this corporate affirmation of welcome where everyone welcomes everyone around them, it is critically important that the handicapped be involved to the full. They are part of the family. By being baptized, by sharing in the symbolic actions of the eucharist and by giving and receiving the 'kiss of peace', individuals may in worship be helped to recognize that they belong and so come to know for themselves the 'good news' of salvation and their fundamental worth as persons whom God loves.

7

Persons are loved as the selves that they are

As noted at the end of the previous chapter, the 'kiss of peace' in the eucharist is an important activity in worship. It does not merely provide a way of marking the acceptance of each other by those taking part. Nor is its significance limited to indicating that the welcome, care and cherishing implicit in this mutual acceptance should be the ideal pattern for the human community in general. The kiss of peace points beyond the worshipping community to the one who is worshipped. It symbolizes God's love for each individual and, thereby, the fundamental ground of their worth. It is thus a dramatic (although as practised in many instances a not very powerful) way of expressing the 'good news' of salvation. Two points, however, need to be borne in mind about the practice and significance of the kiss of peace if it is to be a proper expression of the human community and an authentic symbol of human beings' relationship to God.

The first point is that the kiss of peace must be practised in a way that respects the privacy and dignity of those to whom it is offered. That this may be an unexpected proviso does not mean that it is unimportant. Sometimes people with good motives act in insensitive ways. Persuaded of the value of being a fully-participating member of the community, they fail to be aware that what appeals to them may appear to other people intrusive and even threatening. A loving community needs to be critically self-aware. Among other things this will help its members to recognize that it is wrong for individuals to force themselves on others and to expect everyone to respond in similar ways. This is particularly important when handicapped persons are involved. Physical constraints may make it impossible for them to dodge, and mental handicaps may make it difficult for them to cope with strangers pressing on them 'the kiss of peace'.

Some people have no inhibitions about hugging and being hugged; others may even be embarrassed by a nod of acknowledgement. Those who want to sit quietly by themselves in worship should not be made to feel that they must 'join in'. Personalities and circumstances differ. What is delightful for one person is intrusive for another; what is appropriate at one time is damaging at another. Genuine love cares for the dignity and individuality of those who are loved. Seeing Newman walking on his own, Edward Copleston quoted to him Cicero's 'never less lonely than when alone' (Newman 1956: 36). Congregations who seek to force people into fellowship, like parents who try to jolt their teenage children out of their 'moodiness', need to learn God's respect for the individuality of each person.

The other point is that people should not be regarded as having worth because they are anything other than they actually are. Some classical doctrines of atonement are unacceptable because they employ models that imply a lack of realism in the divine understanding. One of them, for instance, suggests that because of the death of Jesus God pretends that people have qualities which they do not actually have. 'Righteousness', that is, is sometimes treated as a quality which can be 'imputed' to sinners: thus Charles Wesley has believers singing of boldly approaching 'the eternal throne' since they are 'clothed in righteousness divine' (Hymn: 'And can it be'). It makes oneness with God sound like having been given the correct dress to enter the royal enclosure at Ascot – and Jesus as a benefactor who has paid the bill in advance at a divinely appointed Moss Bros!

People do dress up on occasions. Sometimes onlookers may be hoodwinked into thinking that the top hats, morning suits and posh dresses show that those wearing them are important people. God, however, is not tricked. The divine knows the qualities of each individual exactly. The self-centred desires of prodigal sons in leaving home and the selfish hopes that may draw them back when they have squandered their inheritance, as well as the obstinate care of parents and the jealous conceit of sisters and brothers, are all clear to God. As the collect puts it, God is the one 'unto whom all hearts are open, all desires known, and from whom no secrets are hid'.

Nevertheless, while God knows all that there is to be known about each person, it is each person as she or he is whom God loves and who thereby has ultimate worth. The prodigal and the prig are not loved because God thinks that they are other than they are, nor because eventually they may be drawn to love like their father. Each moment they are loved as the persons that they actually are at that moment, and not for what they might become.

This does not mean that God is complacent about a person's state. In loving a psychopath, God is not content with the drives and activities that destroy that self as well as threaten the well-being of others. Even less does the divine love for such persons mean that their demonic urges are endorsed as good. On the contrary, in loving them God desires that the drives and activities of such individuals be changed, whether it be a matter of medical healing or of moral persuasion or of religious repentance, so that their lives may become whole and their activities satisfyingly creative. In this respect change is something that love properly wants for those who are loved. At one extreme such change may take the form of the dramatic restructuring of the personality which has been witnessed to by some; at the other it may have the form of a quiet process of re-formation. Nevertheless, whatever changes are desirable, the individual who is actual now is the one whom God loves now, and in loving gives that self fundamental worth.

In the light of these two points, namely, the importance of respecting the personal preferences of others and the need to appreciate that God loves people as they actually are, we shall in this chapter first suggest some further implications of holding that people have worth as the selves that they are, and then, as promised in earlier chapters, go on to consider the so-called problem of natural evil.

Whether its understanding of salvation is expressed in terms of the classical doctrine of justification by grace through faith or in terms of liberation from all that devalues human existence, theistic faith affirms the freedom of the individual. This freedom has negative and positive aspects.

Negatively it affirms the freedom of individuals from having to be what they are not. Although the root of the word 'religion' may refer to rules that bind people into conformity with a divinely determined pattern of being, authentic faith in God perceives that God is not so minded. To understand God's will for human beings in terms of slavish obedience to arbitrary commands that are imposed on them from without is to confuse the mind of God with the petty authoritarianism asserted by insecure persons. This does not mean, of course, that God – and others – may not point out that certain patterns of behaviour tend to lead to the satisfaction of the proper goal of human existence and that other patterns have the opposite effect. To recommend the former ways and to question the latter, however, will not be to make arbitrary demands on persons. It will rather be more like helping them to recognize the principles for guiding conduct.

The negative aspect of this freedom also means that theistic faith does not require people to pretend to be other than they are. The quiet person is under no obligation to try to be a jolly member of the fellowship; the questioning person does not have to feel guilty about doubting; the humourist does not have to act in a staid manner; the emotional person does not have to try to adopt a stiff upper lip – nor the reserved person to let her or his feelings show. So far as it implies a recognition of the individuality of persons, non-conformity is a proper principle for all Christian bodies. It contradicts itself and the faith which it professes, however, if it turns into a conformist demand not to conform! Freedom means that individuals are to be respected as the persons that they are, not for their readiness and ability to satisfy the requirements of a Procrustean measure of allegedly authentic human being.

The positive aspect of the freedom of the individual affirmed by theistic faith is that persons are liberated by God to explore creatively the potentialities of their existence. Our fundamental worth depends simply and solely upon God's interest in each of us each moment as the persons that we then happen to be. This interest does not wax or wane according to the degree to which the development of our personal being approximates to the details of a divine blueprint for our individual lives. On the contrary, it is an interest that unceasingly promotes our creative self-formation.

This latter point has often, but wrongly, been considered

to be incompatible with the doctrine of creation. Traditionally that doctrine has been understood to maintain that each species, and perhaps each particular natural object, has been specifically determined by God to be what and as it is. John Ray, for example, admires the benevolent wisdom of God which is 'manifested in the works of the creation' – for example, in 'the wonderful Art and Providence of the Contriver and Former of our Bodies' as is shown by the design of our teeth and by the opposition of thumb and fingers (Ray 1722: 240, 267, 278)! From such a doctrine it is appropriate to conclude that human beings only live authentically if they conform to the pattern of being that God intends for them.

It is this implication of the doctrine of God as creator that leads thinkers such as Friedrich Nietzsche and Jean-Paul Sartre to reject God in order to affirm the possibility of authentic human existence. Since the existence of God contradicts the freedom of human beings to choose who they shall be, Nietzsche's 'free spirits' experience 'light, happiness, relief, exhilaration, encouragement, dawn' when they hear 'the news that "the old god is dead"' (Nietzsche 1974: 280). Sartre is less buoyant. He recognizes that people may feel themselves 'forlorn' when they become convinced that there is no God on whom to depend for values and legitimation; nevertheless, the non-existence of God is the condition as well as the cost of being free (Sartre 1948: 34).

Theists may seem to warrant the gravamen of the charge brought against them by Nietzsche and Sartre when they affirm that it is in God's service that they find their 'perfect freedom'. How can those who are obedient to another be perfectly free? The answer is not to be found simply by arguing that since God knows and wills what is the best for each of us, both collectively and individually, to obey God corresponds to satisfying our best interests. That answer is inadequate in itself. It is necessary to make clear what is meant by such obedience. If it is understood as conformity to a set of material commands (like obeying the maker's instructions in operating a machine), then it confirms that we are not free. In that case God provides the instructions for living: our responsibility is to accord with them. If, on the other hand, God's will is understood to be that we should, to a significant extent, be responsible for the character of our being, then we are in a radically different situation. To 'obey' God in this case is to accept the principle that we are responsible for our being. Thrown into existence, condemned to be free, we find that the reality of God, *pace* Sartre, calls us to recognize that 'existence comes before essence' (cf. Sartre 1948: 26, 34), that is, that we are free to choose the character of our being.

It is this latter understanding of the divine will, furthermore, that corresponds to what developments in the natural order indicate about the character of God's activity as creator. Investigations into the way in which natural objects and organisms have evolved make the kind of understanding of divine creativity found in Ray rationally untenable. Things as we find them now are not as they are because God has so designed and produced them – the Bactrian camel with two humps and the dromedary with one, the monkey with a prehensile tail and the human being with an appendix. They are as they now are because that is the current outcome of the interactions of accidental events with regular patterns in the natural order since the original constituents of this planet came together. A similar story apparently applies to the cosmos. Whatever, then, may be the ultimate responsibility of God as creator for the nature of things, the conclusion to be drawn from reflection on that nature is that God's creativity is expressed through 'open-ended' processes. As Arthur Peacocke puts it, in these processes the world's 'potentialities' are explored and actualized; 'new modes of existence' emerge from 'the variations and combinations inherently possible' in the constituents of the world (Peacocke 1979: 210). God as creator does not fix the actual state of all that exists, whether as species or as individuals, according to predetermined patterns; God delights in what evolves through the play of free creativity in the processes of reality (cf. Peacocke 1979: 106ff).

If this interpretation of the doctrine of creation be correct, it is wrong to consider that human freedom is threatened by the status of God as creator. On the contrary, God's creative intention is partly realized through the free creative acts by which human beings give concrete form to their existence. Authentic faith in God does not inhibit but stimulates human creativity by perceiving that God delights in the good which is thereby actualized.

Although the worth of persons does not depend on the value of what they contribute to the divine, but on God's love for them, this does not imply that God is careless about what they produce. The case is, rather, that God enjoys the values realized in all that they do, whether it be the grin of a happy infant or the playing of a Chopin. Furthermore, while for us the memory of past events perishes and their values eventually become unidentifiable parts of the causal influence of the past upon us, each past event is everlastingly remembered and its distinct quality preserved in God. The divine awareness embraces all that happens and loses nothing that it has embraced.

What, however, does this understanding of the compatibility of theistic faith with human freedom imply about the basic character and status of each person as being 'in the image of God'? In spite of much debate in Christian theology, the biblical basis of this metaphor is obscure and its biblical use rare. Nevertheless, the phrase has gained considerable importance in Christian reflection on the doctrine of human being. It is, therefore, appropriate to consider here what might be meant by it as a description of all human beings, including those who are profoundly handicapped. Should, for instance, this theological description of human existence be interpreted as a way of applying to human existence theistic faith's understanding of God as delighting in creativity? If so, human beings will be held to resemble God in being creative.

The unsatisfactory nature of such an interpretation emerges as soon as the actual state of human existence is taken into account. While it may be feasible – although also pretentious – to consider that there is a likeness to God in the creativity of a Michelangelo or an Isaac Newton, the notion that all persons may be justifiably held to be 'in the image of God' because they are creative (at least potentially) appears trivial when we think of the mass of humankind. This is not to deny that each individual each moment makes his or her own response to the environment in which she or he is situated. That is what it is to exist in the processes of reality. On the other hand, the creativity expressed in those responses in most cases in all people, and in practically all cases in most people, is so minimal as to be insignificant. If this is what establishes the status of human beings, then that status is itself trivial. Any attempt to identify the significance of human beings by comparing them with God in this way fails.

This failure becomes even more apparent when the case of severely handicapped people is taken into account. As is the case with all that exists, their lives are sequences of responses to their environments. As is also the case with all persons, those responses are mostly unconscious. We are aware of only a minute portion of the factors affecting us. What distinguishes handicapped people, however, is that the identification of them as being such – that is, as *handicapped* – expresses the judgement (whether justifiable or not) that they are less able than most to make sense of or to respond to their environment. Hence, unless creativity is accidental and the 'values' which it realizes purely random occurrences, their identification as being handicapped persons suggests that their scope for creativity is markedly less than average – and, as was noted earlier, in any case that capacity by itself does not provide a convincing basis for affirming the significance of humankind as being 'in the image of God'.

Even less satisfactory is the attempt to interpret the status of being 'in the image of God' in terms of human rationality, and particularly in terms of the self-awareness which is the condition of moral responsibility. This, however, has not always been appreciated. While, for example, in the *Monologion* Anselm criticizes the analogy between God and an artisan for being 'very incomplete' (Anselm 1962: 58), he asserts that the 'rational mind' not only can investigate the reality of God, but also, by reflecting on its own nature, can become aware of the triune nature of God. He puts it that

> the more earnestly the rational mind devotes itself to learning its own nature, the more effectively does it rise to the knowledge of that Being [God] . . . For, if the mind itself alone among all created beings is capable of remembering and conceiving of and loving itself, I do not see why it should be denied that it is the true image of that being which, through its memory and intelligence and

love, is united in an ineffable Trinity. Or, at any rate, it
proves itself to be the more truly the image of that Being
by its power of remembering, conceiving of, and loving,
that Being . . . Hence, no faculty has been bestowed on
any creature that is so truly the image of the Creator.
(Anselm 1962: 131f)

This evaluation of the theological significance of human
rationality is justified if significant knowledge of the divine
by human beings is allowed to be possible (i.e., if the
description 'ineffable' is taken as a metaphysical compliment
rather than as applying literally to the divine reality). Since
God must be thought of in terms of the highest mode of being
that we are acquainted with (cf. Pailin 1990: 49), this, if
Anselm be correct, is to be found in our awareness of
ourselves as rational beings.

That God may be imaged in terms of the human and, in
particular, in terms of human rationality, does not show,
however, that it is human rationality which identifies
humankind as such as being 'in the image of God'. What
should happen (and generally does happen) when a concept
of God is developed is that those constructing it apply to the
divine those qualities (or that coherent package of qualities)
which, as Anselm puts it in the *Proslogion*, 'it is better to be
than not to be' (Anselm 1962: 11). This means that
theologians should not construct their concept of God from
what is common to all human beings, let alone to all that
exists, but from what they regard as the highest qualities
found in human beings. (And such debates as those about
whether divine compassion involves impassibility or suffering,
and whether divine righteousness is or is not compatible
with divine mercy, show that it is not self-evident to all
theologians which are those 'highest qualities'!)

If, then, the claim that human beings are 'in the image of
God' does not mean that *all* human beings, simply in order to
be classed as properly *human* beings, must have some
qualities from which God may be 'imaged', what is meant by
the claim? This question is particularly pertinent when we
take into account the status of handicapped people as being
'in the image of God'. As was mentioned earlier, what is
considered to justify describing some people as handicapped

(however trivial from the divine perspective may be the sense of superiority entertained by those considering themselves not to be handicapped) is that they are notably restricted in such matters as their capacities for autonomy, creativity and rationality. If to be 'in the image of God' were, then, to be interpreted as referring to the possession of such characteristics, it would seem to follow that handicapped people are themselves only partially or deficiently 'in the image of God'. Alternatively, it might be held that they may still be described as being in that image because, but only because, either on genetic or on social grounds they belong to the class of beings which have those characteristics. While a particular individual may not have all the qualities which satisfy the description, that individual may be deemed to warrant its application to herself or himself because he or she is a member of a class whose members generally – and perhaps typically (but clearly not stereotypically) – do satisfy it.

Such conclusions are to be resisted. This is not simply because they are demeaning to handicapped people and offensive to those who care for them. Nor is it simply because awareness of the finitude of all human beings highlighted by the case of handicapped people makes claims for the status of being 'in the image of God' ludicrous for any human being. What human characteristic is so comparable to the nature of God that any human being can justifiably claim in this respect to be in the image of the divine? Voltaire's story (quoted in chapter four) of a mole and a June bug arguing as to whether it was a big mole or a clever June bug who built the toilet in the garden (Voltaire 1962: 240) ridicules the human pretensions underlying some theologians' discussions about the nature of God! The latter's dullness should not be allowed to camouflage the fact that their questions may not be very far from the child's 'Does God like ice cream as I do?' The apophatic tradition in Orthodox theology which calls the faithful to worship with love that which is profoundly mysterious is an important corrective to Western theology's passion for conceptual specifications of the divine.

What, then, is the significance of holding that all human beings, as such, are 'in the image of God'? A clue might be held to be given by an unusual use of the phrase in Genesis

5.3. Having earlier been told (Genesis 1.27) that God chose to create human beings 'in our image and likeness', the use of the phrase 'in his image and likeness' in Genesis 5.3 might be interpreted as describing a relationship between Adam and his son Seth. From this usage we today, with our very different understanding of what is meant by God as creator, might be led to connect the metaphor of being 'in the image of' with 'belonging to the family of' – and hence with all the privileges that belong to being a member of a family. In the end, however, the biblical use is far from clear. What is important for us is what we are to make of this description. Just as, for example, Alex was born into a particular human family, so, like his father and everyone else in the world, he may be held to be in 'the image of God' because he came into being as part of God's family. To be 'in the image of God', in other words, can be held not to refer to some observable quality by which human beings may be discriminated from other beings, but to announce a status which belongs to persons simply by the accident of their being.

Being 'in the image of God', however, must connote more than simply being a member of a group – the group constituting the 'family of God' – if it is to identify anything in particular in what it is to be 'human'. What, then, does the claim that persons are 'in the image of God' point to in human being? If 'being in the image of' is connected to 'belonging to the family of', what is the 'privilege' that attends being a member of God's family? As has been mentioned, Tillich holds that 'a symbol participates in the reality of that for which it stands' (Tillich 1951: 265). It shares in some ontologically significant way in the quality of the symbolized. This understanding of symbolism gives a further clue to what may be meant by the metaphor of being 'in the image of God'.

Sometimes the reverence given to statues and pictures representing the divine seems to unsympathetic observers to fail to distinguish between the object of worship and its representation. Accusations of idolatry then arise. Missionary propaganda and interdenominational strife has copied Isaiah (cf. Isaiah 44.14ff) in charging those who use images in worship with idolatry. On the other hand, those who appreciate religious sensibility will not be surprised to learn that in a Roman Catholic school, after boisterous pupils had smashed a plaster image, they were offended when a schoolteacher remarked that the fragments would serve well as drainage material for her plantpots, or that a Muslim journal requests those who receive it to dispose of it in a fitting way since it contains quotations from the holy Qur'ān. Of course, plaster is plaster and paper is paper, whether it conveys something sacred or is used in utterly profane ways. Sympathetic understanding of religious awareness recognizes, however, that the distinction between authentic and allegedly idolatrous worship is not clear cut. This is not just because worship is not directed to images and symbols but to that which they represent. It is also because what communicates the divine is felt to be linked to the divine and to become marked by the holiness of the divine. The images and symbols which express the reality of God thus come themselves to be felt to be sacred, even though their sacredness is not intrinsic but derivative.

The treatment of the images and symbols used in worship illuminates what may be meant when human beings are held to be 'in the image of God'. Just as something of the divine holiness rubs off on the symbols and images which function as media by which people become aware of the reality of God, so too something of the holiness of the divine is imparted to human beings by the interest that God has in them. According to this interpretation, it is not an intrinsic quality of human existence that is referred to when people are held to be 'in the image of God', but the status that is given to each person because God is concerned about her or him. In other words, to recognize that people are 'in the image of God' is to recognize that they are touched by the holiness of God. And the grace through which they are so affected is universal. It is not a response to some quality which they genetically inherit (like being a member of a supposedly chosen people), nor a reward for what they achieve (like being morally pure or intellectually creative); it is a consequence of the all-embracing character of God's love.

By pointing to the holiness of each person, the doctrine that people are 'in the image of God' thus emphasizes the God-given significance that belongs to each human being.

The negative side of this significance becomes apparent when the adage 'Hurt my friend and you hurt me' becomes ultimate in the dominical charge, 'Anything you did for one of my brothers here, however humble, you did for me' (Matthew 25.40). Violations of the person are not only morally outrageous and destructive of human society; they are assaults on God. It is not sentimentality, therefore, that justifies the warning, 'Never despise one of these little ones; I tell you, they have their guardian angels in heaven, who look continually on the face of my heavenly Father' (Matthew 18.10). However radically the reference to 'guardian angels' may have to be demythologized, the point is clear: the 'little ones' – and so too those who are in any way handicapped – have God's attention. To harm or to despise them is to blaspheme against the holy.

The holiness that comes to each person as being 'in the image of God' is, however, also to be interpreted positively. It affirms the worth and dignity of each person as known as such by God. When Jürgen Moltmann gave the Samuel Ferguson Lectures at Manchester in 1989, he mentioned in conversation an incident when he was a prisoner-of-war in England after the end of the Second World War. Having been allowed to leave the camp for a few hours, he went to a service at a local church. The minister greeted him and asked him who he was. With the drilled reflexes of a soldier he gave his surname and number. The minister replied, 'No. What is *your* name?' 'Jürgen.' 'That's right. You are Jürgen. Hello. I'm Frank.' It was a revealing encounter. He was no longer a name and number in a military unit. He was a person who had a name of his own. The same is true of every person because she or he is cherished as that person by God. However the world may spurn people or ridicule them or ignore them or devalue them, each individual is known and loved by God. Embraced within the divine being, each person is touched by the holiness of God and is to be respected accordingly.

It is in terms of this understanding of the human that the significance and destiny of people should be considered. This is particularly important when we reflect on the case of handicapped persons. According to traditional interpretations of the Christian hope, death is not the end of a person's existence as a conscious and responsive subject but a passage into a transformed mode of personal being. This understanding has been moulded to a great extent by remarks in Paul's letters to the Corinthians about the resurrection of the dead. He states, for instance, that the earthly body 'is raised imperishable . . . in glory . . . in power . . . as a spiritual body'. At 'the last trumpet-call' both living and dead will be 'changed . . . in the twinkling of an eye' and be 'clothed with immortality' (1 Corinthians 15.42f, 51ff; cf. 2 Corinthians 5.1ff). Although the details of the future state may be obscure, these are powerful metaphors. They are picked up in hymnody. Charles Wesley, for example, writes of entering into 'the promised rest, The Canaan of Thy perfect love' (Hymn: 'God of all power'), and Isaac Watts looks forward to

> . . . a land of pure delight,
> Where saints immortal reign;
> Infinite day excludes the night,
> And pleasures banish pain. (Hymn: 'There is a land')

Behind these descriptions of human destiny, however unsatisfactory developments of them may be, is the conviction that some people at least survive death to enjoy a state of perfect personal existence. Whether all persons (eventually) so survive, or only a restricted group (such as that of 'true believers'), is disputed. What is not disputed is that in order to enjoy this perfect mode of being, persons have to be transformed, whether through a divine act of immediate transfiguration or by a process of amelioration (as in notions of 'purgatory').

In view of this understanding of the future for persons, it is not surprising that some believers have been tempted by the suggestion that while in her or his 'earthly life' a handicapped person may suffer from all kinds of limitations to his or her personal development and creativity, she or he will have in future state a mode of being where all these limitations are removed. The post-mortem existence of handicapped persons is thus treated as something like recovery from an illness. Just as a person may get over a bout of pneumonia and display again the physical and mental vigour which she or he had before the illness, so after death a handicapped person may be expected to be transformed into a state of personal being in which he or she is not handicapped.

The suggestion that this is the fate of handicapped persons is attractive in certain respects. It may be considered to offer hope, even if a distant hope, to those who are frustrated by their handicaps, and comfort to those who care about them. Even if their handicaps cannot be eradicated in this world, they will not characterize the final state of their being. When all are transformed into the likeness of God (cf. 1 John 3.2), there will presumably be no longer any handicapped persons. Whatever the unsatisfactory state of their earthly existence, eventually they will have the perfect mode of being which God wills for everyone. It seems an attractive prospect. There are, however, grounds for considering this suggestion to be a temptation which should be resisted. Its attractiveness turns out to be illusory.

One possible objection to this suggestion is not restricted to the case of handicapped persons, although their supposed post-mortem destiny highlights the issue in an acute way. The nub of this objection applies to all cases of post-mortem existence, especially when it is interpreted in a certain way. Basically it is the problem of the identity of the individual in the post-mortem state. According to a widespread evangelical understanding of the Christian faith, after death persons are raised in a state of perfection (or in a state appropriate to the heavenly realm of the presence of God). This raises a problem. And, so far as the problem arises in relation to the future state of handicapped people, it does not matter whether the evangelical doctrine is held to describe the destiny of every person or whether, as in most traditional understandings of Christian belief, it is restricted to those who die 'in a state of grace', whoever they may be. Whichever be the case, the problem can be put as the following question: *Who* is the person who is raised?

In the case of a few people (the saints), it may be that the difference in personal character between the person who died and the perfect person who is raised to post-mortem existence is so minimal that no greater problems of identity arise than when we wake after a night's sleep. In the morning

I never doubt that I am the same 'me' who went to sleep the night before. Admittedly there will have been physiological and mental changes during the night, but the overlap between the two states is too massive to evoke even a momentary doubt unless I am playing games of philosophical scepticism! A little worrying might be the situation on recovery from a prolonged illness, especially one in which my self-awareness had been seriously impaired or distorted for a considerable time. If I were to awake from a coma or recover from a massive mental disease, I might initially have problems in relating myself to the person who fell ill. The claim that I have 'recovered' (whether made by myself or by others about me) would, however, probably depend to some extent on the recovery of my memory of 'my' past states and hence of my sense of identity as a developing person.

More worrying would be the case of an individual who started to suffer from mental disease when a young adult, lived fifty more years in a confused state, and then recovered clarity of mind. Who in that case would be the person who has recovered? If it is the 'person' who lived before the disease struck, what is the significance of 'the person' who lived for fifty years in the fogs of dementia? Does that personal existence count for nothing? Is 'recovery' in such a case to be understood as the continuity of a self-identifying individual, or as the reconstruction of a 'person' who faded out as the effects of the disease developed, or as the emergence of a new person? Whichever answer is preferred, it is hard to defend the claim that the person who is now well is the same person who was taken ill.

If the case of the person recovering from dementia is worrying, much more worrying is the evangelical claim that a person who dies in a state of grace, however great their sins have been, is raised in a state of perfection. The basic problem here is not that of how one would identify oneself as being the 'same' person as the one who died if, as Paul suggests, one's earthly body were exchanged for a spiritual one (think of the crisis of identity that I would suffer if I found a radically different kind of 'face' looking at me in the heavenly equivalent of a mirror when I became self-conscious again!), although this is not a minor problem. Bodily continuity is what generally anchors our sense of identity. The basic problem, at least in my case, would be my self-recognition as being the same person who died if the self that became conscious after death were in a state of spotless perfection. While not desiring to boast about my imperfections, I suspect that if I were now to die and such a transformation were to happen, the discontinuity between the self that died and the perfect self that was raised from the dead would make it more plausible to hold that a new self had been created than that the transformed self continued the subjective identity of the self who had died. Even if the self that became conscious in a post-mortem existence had inherited the memories of my present self, it is questionable if they would justify claims to identity. Since they would be memories that the perfect self would apprehend and evaluate very differently than I now do, in important respects (namely, as contributing to the being of that self as a person) they would not be the same memories.

Such problems become even more acute if we consider the identity of a severely handicapped person on being raised in a state of perfection (i.e., without being handicapped) after dying. If this means that the handicaps which moulded that person's earthly existence would no longer affect her or him, in what way is it the 'same' person? It seems that while there might be some inherited characteristics, the gulf between the earthly and the post-mortem modes of personal existence is such that it is more appropriate to say that a new person has come to be than that the previous self has undergone a transformation that can justifiably be compared to recovery from an illness.

The problem of the identity of the self who dies with the post-mortem perfect self may not, however, be an insuperable objection to the suggestion that in their subjective post-mortem existence those whom we know as handicapped will no longer be hampered. It may be possible to overcome it by putting forward something akin to the doctrine of purgatory – the notion of a process of amelioration in which individuals change into the desired state over a period of time during which they retain their sense of identity as developing persons. If the main reasons for objecting to such a notion turn out to be evangelical impatience with the length of the process required and horror at the effort that might well be demanded, it can be ignored as trivial and selfish.

A more significant objection to the suggestion that handicapped persons will cease to be handicapped in the post-mortem state is that it applies to their future post-mortem existence a judgement which, as has previously been pointed out, is questionable in terms of their present life. What is objectionable in this judgement is its assumption that notions of human destiny which involve post-mortem transformation can be given material content by applying to them what we consider to be the nature of fulfilling existence for us in this life.

Such an assumption makes the kind of error which distorts some liberation theologies produced in the First World. In the latter case it is the error of assuming that the deprived and oppressed people of the Third World are such because they lack the wealth, material goods and supposed social, political and economic freedoms that people in the First World generally consider to be universally desirable. It is often overlooked that those who consider these things desirable have been culturally conditioned to value them highly and to enjoy them. More critical appraisal may reveal that some of these supposed 'goods' oppress people in the First World and vitiate the thought of theologians who are conditioned by its culture. If this turns out to be the case, the liberation theologians of the First World need themselves to be liberated from the false values which they presuppose through cultural indoctrination before they presume to instruct those in other cultures and regimes about the proper goals of human existence.

Similarly, those who assert that handicapped persons will be liberated from their handicaps in a post-mortem existence must not uncritically assume that what they want and enjoy in life is what those whom they regard as handicapped would or should desire. It may be that the lives of the latter are not always deficient because they do not share the things that the former consider important. In my own case, for example, I have friends who do not consider that their lives lack anything because they are not disturbed by the intellectual puzzles that fascinate me. Indeed, the type of mind which I find stimulating and desirable, they perceive as a source of

unattractive worries. Why should I judge their quality of life
to be less than mine? Furthermore, which is the better basis
for imagining post-mortem existence? Will the brain-teasing
character of existence continue there or will all become clear?
If the latter be the case, what I have thought to be good will
no longer characterize existence. On the other hand, as a
musical idiot, I find images of heavenly choirs positively
depressing. To sing everlastingly would be hell for me and
disaster for those near me!

These trivial illustrations remind us that we should be
cautious in using our culturally moulded self-understanding
as the clue to understanding the proper nature of human
existence and of its destiny. Although we cannot reach such
understanding except by reflecting on our own experience of
it, we must be cautious in claiming that what we regard as
handicaps must necessarily be such. We must remember, as
has already been pointed out, that we are all finite and that
the differences between those who are considered to be
handicapped and those who are not may not be significant
from the divine point of view.

This point leads to the fundamental objection to the
suggestion that in a post-mortem existence those who are
handicapped in this life will exist in a state that is freed from
such limitations. It is the objection that such a suggestion
threatens, if it does not actually deny, the divine love for the
actual individual, however handicapped that person may be.
The divine care for each individual is the affirmation of each
person as that person. It does not 'unself' the actual
individual by loving her or him for what she or he might be
or eventually will be. In loving and thereby giving value to
each person, God accepts and cherishes each person as she
or he actually is. Whatever transformations may occur as a
person grows in holiness or moves into a different mode of
existence, it is essentially *that* person as he or she is at the
present moment, and not a different one or a potential one,
who is embraced in the divine.

Furthermore, it is arguable that just as in some post-
mortem state I would not be 'me' if I did not question and
could sing in tune, so others would lose their individuality if
their peculiarities, including their limitations, were eradicated.
If post-mortem existence were to involve transformations

which result in the elimination of differences, what once were distinct individuals would become indistinguishable items. In that case the result would not be the perfecting of persons, whatever that may imply. It would be their destruction.

Such a fate is neither the realization of God's love for us nor the fulfilment of faith's hope. It contradicts them. While, therefore, it may seem comforting to those who love a handicapped person to believe that after death that person will enjoy a state of being which is not so limited, such a belief is mistaken if and in so far as it implies that the handicapped person does not have worth to God as the particular person whom we know here and now. It is that person, not some potential person who may come to exist in the future, who has worth, because it is that person whom God loves – and as that person.

Before this discussion of hope and human destiny ends, it should be noted that the preceding remarks have assumed the validity of the belief that human beings continue to exist as experiencing and responding persons after death. This belief, however, is open to question. While it is not appropriate in this study to discuss the issue of subjective immortality at any length, it should be noted that the belief that we survive our deaths is not a necessary implication of faith in God as one who loves us. The persons whom God loves now are you and me and everyone else as they are now, not as we once were (although then God loved us as the persons we were then) nor as we may become (although God will then love us as the persons we then will be). If, therefore, we are finite beings, God loves each of us as such.

The desire to have subjective immortality may stem among other things from a desire to be like God in a way that is not appropriate to our finitude rather than from insight into the nature of our being as those who are loved by God. If this be so, our true immortality may not lie in continued existence as experiencing and responding subjects but in the everlasting preservation in the divine awareness of each moment of our actual experiences as persons with a finite span of existence. Our destiny in that case is not 'subjective' but 'objective immortality' in the all-embracing reality of the divine.

When Alex's father read the draft of this passage, he asked

me if 'objective immortality' could be said to be what Rupert
Brooke is referring to in 'The Soldier' when, in the second
stanza, he writes:

> And think, this heart, all evil shed away,
> A pulse in the eternal mind, no less
> Gives somewhere back the thoughts by England given.
>   (Brooke 1942: 150)

If this is the meaning of 'objective immortality', it seemed to
him that to say that someone becomes 'a pulse in the eternal
mind' is not an adequate way of claiming that a person was
immortal. I agree. The metaphor of being a 'pulse' (and,
incidentally, the Platonic notion of the soul) lacks the
recognition of the significance of the individual self as a
personal being in relationship to God that a satisfying notion
of immortality requires. This recognition is not, however,
lacking from the notion of 'objective immortality' as I use it
here. What is incorporated into the divine reality are not
impersonal quanta of experienced feelings (whatever they
might be) that become part of what God is rather like the
way in which the energy which I generate in exercising is
dissipated into the atmosphere. God takes into the divine all
the experiences (including the experiences of thinking) that
constitute each person as that particular person and preserves
them without loss as the memory of the individual self that
was loved by God each moment of her or his life and will be
everlastingly cherished by God as that person. The moments
of the self, furthermore, continue to influence each present
(cf. Brooke's 'gives somewhere back'), but this influence is in
and through their embodiment in the influencing presence of
the reality of God as a constituent factor of each moment of
reality (cf. Whitehead 1978: xiiif; Hartshorne 1962: 245ff;
Pailin 1986: 181ff for more on this view).

In any case, whatever be the credibility of notions of
subjective immortality and post-mortem transformation into
the likeness of God, the ultimate worth of each person is in
being cherished and embraced by God. Persons are not loved
by God for what they were, nor for what others have done for
them, nor for what they may become in the future, nor for
what they may be in a transformed post-mortem mode of
being. They are loved now as they are now. If subjective

immortality be considered to be a true perception of human destiny with God, it is misunderstood if it is thought to devalue the God-given worth of each moment of a person's life before death.

In the case of Alex, for instance, it should be recognized that God loved Alex every moment of Alex's life, and that after his death God has cherished and will for ever continue to cherish each of Alex's experiences. God's love for Alex was not then and is not now because of what Alex may (have) become through some process of transformation. God loved and loves Alex as Alex actually was each moment.

The divine love is not a love that has ulterior motives, looking beyond the present to what might emerge in the future or to what may be gained in return. It is love for what actually *is* in its *is*ness, as well as love which seeks to influence future states of each self to use the data from the past in the most enriching way that is possible. As Whitehead puts it, in one respect God's love 'does not look to the future; for it finds its own reward in the immediate present'. In another respect the divine love is expressed in 'the patient operation' of caring influence in which God is 'the poet of the world, with tender patience leading it by his vision of truth, beauty, and goodness'. He sums up the love of God for the world thus:

> It is the particular providence for particular occasions. What is done in the world is transformed into a reality in heaven, and the reality in heaven passes back into the world. By reason of this reciprocal relation, the love in the world passes into the love in heaven and floods back again into the world. In this sense, God is the great companion – the fellow-sufferer who understands. (Whitehead 1978: 343, 346, 351)

It is this love that embraced Alex from the moment when he came to be, and will embrace him for evermore.

Furthermore, if there be subjective immortality and accordingly Alex continues to exist as a subject after his death, it is the Alex that his parents and friends knew and loved during his life with them. That is the person who Alex was and is. Neither his selfhood nor that of anyone else is identifiable in terms of the Platonic notion of an unchanging 'soul' which is independent of and unaffected by the individual's existential states. In so far, therefore, that Alex's personhood was inescapably channelled by his handicaps, for they were part of the fundamental structure of being Alex, so they may be expected to continue to mould his subjective immortality. On the other hand, what Newman says about life 'here below' also applies (*pace* Newman) to personal being in what he calls the 'higher world', namely, that 'to live is to change, and to be perfect is to have changed often' (Newman 1890: 40). Thus, just as persons develop in this life, so, if there be some form of post-mortem existence as subjects, they may be expected in that state to develop further. Whatever such changes produce, however, in Alex's case they will be what are appropriate to the person of Alex.

Finally, in considering the significance of human destiny and hope in relation to those who are handicapped, it should be noted that the problematic question of subjective immortality is not the most important issue. More important than questions about surviving death is the recognition that in a real sense death is liberating for every person. Whether or not we continue as subjects in some post-mortem mode of existence, we are incorporated each moment into the all-inclusive richness of the divine reality. There every experience that constitutes us as the persons who we are is for ever remembered and cherished by God as part of God's own being. This is the origin of our worth, the imperishable destiny of our experiences and the ground of our hope.

Is, however, this faith in God credible in view of the evil that exists in the world? This is the final topic for this chapter. In *The Brothers Karamazov* Dostoyevsky confronts the reader with the senselessness of the sufferings of some children. Having reported terrible incidents, Ivan protests that nothing, not even 'the entire truth', is 'worth such a price'. Whatever 'higher harmony' may be secured by such pains does not warrant the cost. And vengeance would not help expiate the evils. It would only increase human suffering. Ivan does not want 'any more suffering'. He wants to 'embrace' all. Therefore he renounces the 'higher harmony altogether' because 'of the love' which he bears to humankind. He returns to God his 'ticket of admission'. In his judgement 'we cannot afford to pay so much' (Dostoyevsky 1964: 274f).

Ivan's stories and his appalled love for humankind are disturbing for those who have faith in God. They make it clear that the problem of suffering is no mere puzzle for intellectual trifling. In the century of Stalin, Hitler and Pol Pot the problem challenges the credibility of theistic faith. If there be a God, why are these things allowed to happen? Why does God not prevent them? Why does God not intervene? Why? Belief turns into a puzzled cry. Can it be that God is not really loving? Ivan does not deny that there is a God; but he refuses to accept the world as God, according to faith's traditional self-understanding, has ordered it.

Ivan backs his response to God by stories about evil due to human cruelty. For others natural evils provoke even greater doubts about the divine. Nothing seems to be able to justify what happens to many people through natural processes.

The problem which evil in general and suffering in particular poses for faith in God is as old as that faith. It is also an issue which should not be dodged in such a study as this. Consequently, before we conclude these reflections on the theology of human being we must, as was promised earlier, consider what may be affirmed in response to the problem of evil. Human suffering, and especially the suffering occasioned by natural processes, challenges the faith of those who believe that the worth of human being is grounded in the all-embracing and inexhaustible love of God. If it be true that God loves each individual, why, they wonder, does God not prevent the sufferings which natural processes as well as human actions inflict on people?

In chapter three it was pointed out that the theological problem posed by the condition of handicapped people is not in itself a form of the problem of suffering. Nevertheless, some handicapped people do suffer, sometimes severely, as a consequence of their handicaps. Others suffer deeply in sympathy and concern as they care for those who are handicapped. Alex, for example, on occasions experienced great discomfort; his parents and others suffered as their love for him was actualized in compassion and concern and, eventually, in sorrow. He suffered helplessly and he could not understand what was happening to him. Those who loved him suffered because the only help which they could give him was so limited. As his mother said some time after Alex had died, 'Those were experiences which I would not want anyone at all ever to have to go through.' Is there, however, any way of reconciling such situations with faith in God as one who loves each individual intimately and totally?

Those who suggest that post-mortem delights can and will compensate for the agonies which some people suffer in this world do not understand the problem. They are insensitive to what actually happens to some people. Notions of adequate future compensation are legal fictions in an unconvincing attempt to camouflage the enormity of the problem.

Just as post-mortem delights could never recompense the tortured children described by Ivan Karamazov, so future wholeness, even if it were compatible with personal identity, could never justify the sufferings which result from the condition of some handicapped people in this life. Thus even if it were credible to hold that in a state of subjective immortality handicapped persons will be totally liberated from their handicaps, no such future state could ever justify their state in this life. Furthermore, if it be good for them to be liberated, then why is it not good for them to be liberated in this life? And if it would be good for them to be liberated in this life, is it still reasonable to hold that God loves them? These questions indicate that reference to post-mortem wholeness does not solve the problem but adds to it.

God is believed to be powerful, wise and benevolent. If the physical, mental and emotional sufferings that attend certain handicaps are evils which it is good to eradicate, God's apparent failure to intervene to prevent people being so handicapped is claimed by some to show that affirmations of the divine love are expressions of pious wishes rather than descriptions of the fundamental character of the real world in which we actually live. Consequently, even though being handicapped is not to be judged to be evil in itself, but as merely an obvious form of the finitude which characterizes all human existence, the problem of evil still confronts theistic understanding of human existence in general and of handicapped people in particular. It is not tenable to maintain that, since all human beings are finite and so in some respects handicapped, there is no theological problem here. How, then, may faith in God respond to the problem of evil?

As has previously been mentioned, one classical attempt to find a solution to the problem of evil holds that suffering due to natural processes is the result of and a punishment for sin. The lack of correlation between what individuals actually suffer and what they seem to merit (for some apparent saints suffer torments and some apparent evil-doers live in luxury) may be 'explained' by holding that humanity inhabits a 'fallen' world. Individuals may thus suffer not because of their own sins but because they are members of a sinful humanity. Another classical solution maintains that suffering due to natural processes is part of the obstacle course that people are set in this life in order to develop and refine their characters. Suffering provides opportunities for the sufferer to discover inner resources to overcome it, and for others to realize their compassion and ingenuity in giving support. If, therefore, we protest to God about suffering, we condemn ourselves: either we are refusing to accept our deserved punishment and our solidarity with humankind or we show that we are failing to cope with our tests.

Neither of these supposed solutions to the problem of evil, however ingeniously developed and however strongly endorsed by the theologically great, is satisfactory. When their implications are clarified, they present God as a being who is not worthy of worship. It is not justifiable to hold that Alex's sufferings were either deserved or educationally helpful to his personal development. Equally unacceptable are claims that they are acceptable as his unfortunate lot in a human situation which overall is socially deserved (as punishment) or desirable (as challenges).

Such responses to the problem of evil are morally and theistically outrageous. The supposed moral principles which are alleged to support them are abhorrent. No good was preserved or upheld by hurting Alex. A being who sanctioned, let alone inflicted, such suffering would be an object of disgust. Such a being might be feared, but could not be worshipped and adored. If the ultimate reality deliberately behaved in such a way, the honest response would be to apply to it John Stuart Mill's remark that 'nearly all the things which men are hanged or imprisoned for doing to each other, are nature's every day performances . . . and in a large proportion of cases, after protracted tortures such as only the greatest monsters whom we read of ever purposely inflicted on their living fellow-creatures' (Mill 1874: 28f). Consequently, although the above solutions to the problem of evil have influential supporters (cf. Hick 1968 for details), I am uncertain whether theists should reject them as atheistic (because they deny the reality of God as a proper object of worship) or condemn them as blasphemous (because they accuse God of such appalling behaviour)!

A third alleged solution argues that the essential nature of the divine not only entails that God must necessarily exist but also that God must exist as the perfect being who is the creative ground of all else. Accordingly, whatever may appear to be the case, what exists must exist in and as part of the best of all possible worlds. One way of developing this doctrine concludes that everything that happens to be must therefore be good in itself, whether it be Alex's smile or the last despairing state of a girl crushed under a collapsed building after an earthquake. This conclusion is not tenable. Some things that occur are bad. To assert that rational reflection shows that they *must* be good is unconvincing: hard experience makes it clear that there must be something wrong with the argument.

The basic argument behind this third solution is, however, also compatible with a different appreciation of what happens in the world. It may be concluded that what in principle is 'the best possible world' that God, as ultimate and perfect, *must* create is one that contains freedom and is structured by natural laws that combine regularity with accidental interactions. If this is how the relationship of the creator to the creation is to be understood, then faith in God's perfection is not necessarily undermined by cases of suffering. They may be held to be 'merely' accidental consequences of the way things happen in the openness essential to the world's being the best possible world.

This latter form of the third solution has much to commend it. It seems based on a rationally defensible analysis of what is implied by the concept of God as the totally adequate object of worship. The problem of evil, however, may then emerge as empirical counter-evidence which challenges the credibility of what is in principle a sound argument from the concept of God. The argument supporting this solution may, that is, be attacked along the following lines. While it is allowed that the argument from the concept of God is convincing in principle, it is suggested that unfortunately in practice we sometimes find that reality does not fit our concepts. This is such a case. The evidence of evil in the world shows, according to the critic of this solution, that the conclusion of the argument does not describe the state of the real world in which we actually live. In reply defenders of this solution may protest that we are not in a position to judge that this is not the 'best possible world'. The evil in the world may be regrettable but in principle its possibility cannot be avoided if the world is to be 'the best possible'. Those who reject this solution and its defence may, furthermore, be accused of lacking wholehearted faith in God. Is this counter-attack a justifiable defence? Or is the question of the alleged doubter the cry of a faith that is seeking to escape outworn forms in order to find the truth about God?

So far as I can judge there is at present no clear conclusion to this debate. There are, however, two ways of responding to it. One of them is classical and finally unsatisfactory. The other is potentially fruitful but seems generally ignored in the debates about the credibility of theistic faith in face of the evil that occurs in the world.

The first response is that presented by the book of Job. It is a response which is similar to that used to defend the second form of the 'the best possible world' argument. As was mentioned earlier in this study, after the debates with his friends about why he suffers as he does, Job is finally confronted with the reality of God. He then perceives that the only adequate 'answer' to the problem of evil is to recognize that there is no answer that human beings can grasp. God's ways are beyond human understanding. Consequently, overwhelmed by the otherness of the holy one and challenged to justify his attempt to demand an answer from God, Job confesses:

I put my finger to my lips . . .
I know that thou canst do all things

and that no purpose is beyond thee.
But I have spoken of great things which I have not
  understood,
things too wonderful for me to know.
I knew of thee then only by report,
but now I see thee with my own eyes.
Therefore I melt away;
I repent in dust and ashes. (Job 40.4; 42.2–6)

The 'answer' of faith according to Job is thus to have faith in God.

Presumably this answer is completely satisfying for any who, like Job in the story, are (or have been) faced with the reality of God. As with Thomas in the post-resurrection story, they have encountered evidence which dissolves their doubts like the sun on the morning mist. Who, however, have such experiences? Those who think that they do presumably are not worried about faith and are not likely to feel a need to read books like this. They *know* – even though others like me may carpingly wonder if they only think that they know! In contrast, I at any rate am more interested in the situation of those whom Jesus referred to when, after commenting on Thomas' confession, he said, 'Happy are they who never saw me and yet have found faith' (John 20.29). What can be said to them (and to me)? How can they find the happiness of faith in God when they are inescapably aware of the evidence of evil in the world?

The conclusion reached by the book of Job, namely that we are to stop questioning and simply believe, is not a persuasive option in a secularist culture. In the current climate of opinion it is easier to hold that 'There is no God' than to hold that 'There is a God but the ways of the divine are inscrutable.' Furthermore, so far as our actual existence is concerned, there seems to be no appreciable difference between the two assertions. As David Hume asks, how do those 'who maintain the absolute incomprehensibility of the Deity, differ from sceptics or atheists, who assert, that the first cause of All is unknown and unintelligible?' (Hume 1935: 195).

If theistic faith is to be a significant as well as a credible way of understanding the processes of reality, what it affirms about God must make sense of the world as we find it to be. This does not mean that it must assume that the present state of affairs is what finally should be and, according to faith's hope, will be. Such an assumption makes the error of regarding the caterpillar rather than the butterfly as the final state of an egg. Faith's understanding of God thus has to combine what makes sense of our real world now with what makes sense of our justifiable perception of God's final end for the processes of reality. It is a tricky combination to achieve – and helps explain why 'faith's understanding' is a matter of 'faith' as well as of 'understanding'. Nevertheless, while hope about what is to be is involved in its understanding, theism can only be rationally credible if it has an appropriate degree of what Ian Ramsey described as 'empirical fit' (cf. Ramsey 1964: 17, 38–40).

This means that the usual way of treating the problem of evil in theology is mistaken. What generally happens is that theologians concerned to establish the rational credibility of theism start by presenting arguments in its favour (sometimes by reference, among other things, to states and events which they interpret as evidence of divine purpose and benevolence in the natural order). When this has been done they *then* attempt to deal with (perhaps it would be more accurate to say 'to explain away') the apparent counter-evidence of certain states and events (namely, those that pose the problem of evil) which apparently do not fit the theistic case. A more convincing theological method would consider all the evidence (both that which supposedly points to purpose and benevolence and the apparent counter-evidence of evil) as parts of the mix of empirically observed states which theistic understanding must take into account from the start.

These remarks about theological method introduce the second, potentially fruitful way of responding to the problem. This response questions the assumptions behind the alleged problem of evil. It points out that the problem is generally posed, and answers to it sought, on the basis of assumptions about divine creativity that are not rationally credible.

It seems to be generally overlooked in discussions about the problem of natural evil that the problem is posed in a way that presupposes a view of the activity of God as creator that is pre-Darwinian and, in its spirit, probably even pre-Copernican. It is assumed, that is, that the objects, structures and processes which we find in nature are as they are because this is how God intended, designed and produced them. The creator is thus deemed to be responsible for all that is – from the speed of light to the gravitational relationship between masses, from the elephant to the flea, from the ordering of galaxies to the behaviour of the quark, and from the reproductive methods of animals to the structure of an influenza virus. As a result of this understanding of what is implied by the status of God as creator, natural evils raise the question of why God, as benevolent, omnipotent and wise, should have included in the creation objects, structures amd processes that cause suffering. Since God is responsible for their reality, there is a problem – a huge problem and, in the judgement of many, so far an apparently insoluble problem – of reconciling God's performance as creator with what is believed about the divine. This is the question of 'theodicy'. It is the question of how to vindicate the ways of God in face of natural evils. Why did God create what causes suffering? Such a question, however, is *mal posée*. It is the wrong question to ask because it presupposes a notion of divine creativity which is no longer rationally tenable.

What theological understanding of God and the world primarily needs is not an answer to the problem of evil as traditionally posed but an understanding of God as creator which makes sense of God's relationship to the actual processes of reality as discovered through scientific investigations. In order to achieve such understanding theologians should not try to make sense of the world as created by God first by deriving a story from its apparently beneficial parts and then seeking to explain away the other parts which do not fit. Instead they should attempt to produce a doctrine of creation that makes sense of everything in the world as we find it to be. When this is done, if it can be done, then the so-called problem of evil will have disappeared. If, on the other hand, it is found to be impossible to produce such a doctrine, then theism as a way of understanding reality (as contrasted, for example, with theistic faith as an expression of human hopes imposed upon an indifferent reality) will cease to be credible.

It is not possible to develop here the details of a doctrine of creation which may satisfy the proper requirements of theological understanding. All that can be offered is a very brief indication of its basic characteristics (for more details, cf. Peacocke 1979; 1986; 1990; Pailin 1989: chapters 7 and 8). It is a doctrine which recognizes that evolutionary change occurs in the natural order largely through processes in which accidental events alter regular patterns. For organic beings this occurs at the level of replications in the DNA and RNA macromolecules, the order of whose nucleotides provides the codes which determine genetic inheritance. It is a process which Jaques Monod describes in terms of 'chance and necessity' (cf. Monod 1972): while the structure of the macromolecules is exactly replicated in nearly every case (so that Monod can speak of 'necessity'), very occasionally some accident (perhaps due to the random incidence of a particle of radiation) creates a change in the order of the nucleotides (hence 'chance'). While the resulting evolutionary process wanders aimlessly up many blind alleys for every fruitful development which happens, it is the accumulative effect of such changes over millions of years that has resulted in the emergence of the living beings that we currently find on this planet, including ourselves.

If this is what scientific understanding discerns to be the character of the processes of reality whose current result is the present cosmos, what may theological understanding affirm about the activity of God as creator? Some thinkers, including Monod, find no role for the divine in the story. For them the story of reality is atheistic. Furthermore, the long history of disappearing gaps which previous thinkers have plugged with 'God' makes theologians who are aware of the history of the interaction between science and religion since Newton's day very chary of alleging that the story of the processes of reality does contain elements that make sense by postulating divine activity. Many are even chary of holding that reality only finds wholeness, and its story completeness, by reference to God.

Nevertheless, while the pattern of natural processes

involved in cosmic and terrestrial evolution does not entail the notion of God in the way that classical natural theologians from Ray to Paley argued, theists may make three points in defence of their understanding. The first is that the story of reality as a whole is unsatisfactorily incomplete without reference to God as the ground of its being, purpose and value. The second point is that the activity of the creator in the processes of reality is not to be seen as the construction of particular processes and entities but rather is to be envisaged in terms of a general pressure towards localized concentration, complexification and novelty through the varying combinations of fundamental forces, and, at the level of the organic, towards the development of macro-molecular structures. The influence of the divine on individual processes is not to be modelled on the intervention of a superior agent – a divine 'hand' that steps in to change things like children changing the pattern of lines in their electric train set. It is more like the influence of the environment on the entities within it.

One possible model for the creative activity of God is the so-called 'trickle-down effect' according to which, in certain systems, the nature of the 'whole' affects as well as is affected by what happens in its constituent parts. A familiar example of this is the way that a person who is persistently 'out of sorts', under great pressure at work and at home and poorly adjusted to people around, may develop physiological problems such as hypertension (high blood pressure), indigestion and ulcers. In some way or other the state of the whole produces an effect in a particular organ of the body. More appealing illustrations are the way that after a dull and dismal winter a bright spring day with clumps of daffodils and leaping lambs invigorates our organs, and the way that the support of friends and the atmosphere of watching crowds can draw out of athletes strengths of which they were not aware. Although there are important differences, at least of degree and maybe also of kind, between the reactions of persons and those of natural processes, the way in which wholes affect their parts and the way in which surrounding situations influence those within them may provide models, although only indirect and tentative models, of the way in which God influences the processes of reality.

The third point which theists may make about their understanding of God as creator is that the divine creativity finds expression through the processes of reality. God does not design and produce specific genera, let alone species or individuals. There is no set of cosmic blueprints according to which God guides the emergence of specific objects or even specific classes of objects. Rather, God's creativity is seen in the general fermentation of the processes of reality and in the appreciative reception of what emerges from them through accident and the random interaction of ordered processes. The natural order has a freedom and indeterminacy which God respects and whose products God enjoys. This does not mean that the processes of reality are purposeless, but that the underlying purpose is the formal one of fostering those processes to develop novel forms and thereby to actualize fresh expressions of aesthetic value. It is a purpose that in at least one place in the cosmos, the earth, has resulted in the emergence of persons able to be aware of this purpose and self-consciously responsive to the divine.

If this understanding of God's creativity is on the right lines (and I recognize that this brief outline leaves much that needs to be worked out, particularly in relation to the way in which God actually influences the processes of reality), it is not justifiable to ask – in terms, say, of a particular influenza virus – 'What was the divine purpose in making this?' The reason why that virus exists is that certain organisms happen to have evolved in that way. It is not because, perhaps in a moment of sadism or as a matter of bored interest, God decided that there should be that particular kind of organism, designed it and brought about its emergence in the world.

It follows from this view of the world and God that it is not justifiable to sing (in sexist language!) 'He's got the whole world in his hands' as if God is a puppeteer who manipulates all that happens by invisible strings. Neither the emergence of specific genera nor the appearance of particular species nor the actuality of each individual creature has come about because God has determined that it should. On the other hand, while this view of God and the world fundamentally modifies traditional theistic understanding of God's creativity, it outlines a view of God as creator which can be regarded as credible in view of the discovered character of the world and also as appropriate to faith in God as the living God whose personal character is for Christians normatively revealed in the story of Jesus.

In the end, then, the proper response to the question why Alex was handicapped and suffered as he did is that it did not happen because God so willed it. God is not a monster. It happened because that was the way in which Alex's genetic make-up happened to be initially constituted and he later developed. His handicaps and the conditions from which he suffered – and all the other cases of natural evil in the world – were no more specifically designed and produced by God than my baldness or the plumage of a robin. What is important in theistic understanding is not to invent a comforting answer to pseudo-questions about why God did this or allowed that to happen. What is important is to recognize that God loved Alex each moment of his being as the person who Alex then was, and that it is this person, the real Alex, who is still cherished by God and will for ever be embraced as a cherished part of the divine reality. And the same is true of every other person.

8

'Be not afraid'

In 1988 Richard Hanson, scholar, bishop, emeritus professor and former colleague, finished his *magnum opus* on the Arian controversy, was elected a Fellow of the British Academy, and was presented with a *Festschrift* written by colleagues and friends. He also discovered that he was suffering from cancer. Not long after he had undergone a major operation I was allowed to pay him a brief visit. Wrapped in his episcopal cloak, he greeted me and then said, 'When I went into hospital, I reflected that I hold a trinitarian faith: I believe that I am in the Father, Christ is in me, and the Spirit is everywhere. Therefore, realizing this, I relaxed. My faith has upheld me.'

It was a moving testimony. It not only gave him an opportunity to challenge what he may well have suspected to be a rather uncertain commitment on my part to credal orthodoxy on this matter! It also allowed him to show that recognition of the trinitarian nature of the divine is much more than a matter of doctrinal wrangling. A proper acknowledgement of the mystery of God, such as is attempted in trinitarian doctrine, has fundamental and practical significance for the lives of those whose faith is in God.

Richard Hanson was correct if he suspected that I am not happy with traditional ways of expressing the doctrine of Trinity such as are contained in the Athanasian creed. Granted that this kind of credal statement is primarily to be interpreted negatively (that is, as rejecting certain erroneous views) rather than as a positive description of the divine, and granted that 'person' in this doctrine is not used in the post-Enlightenment sense of personal identity but means something closer to the notion of the role played by an actor, I am still left puzzled by classical expressions of this doctrine. It is not that I judge that they are clearly wrong. I am not in a position to make such a judgement. My problem is that I am far from clear about precisely what they mean. Consequently

I prefer simply to talk about 'God' (and even that is far from simple; cf. Pailin 1990: especially 42ff) and to leave to others speculations about the internal structure of the Godhead – if that is what the doctrine of the Trinity describes.

If, however, the doctrine of the Trinity, properly interpreted, affirms that the relationship between God and the world is what was outlined in Richard Hanson's testimony as I understand it, then I happily – and wholeheartedly – endorse it. It is a way of expressing a relationship which I find more satisfactorily expressed in the concept of 'panentheism' where what may be called the personal character of the 'God' of this form of theistic belief is held to be normatively perceived through reflection on the life of Jesus as the Christ. Whereas classical understanding of God has tended to imply that God is fundamentally cut off from worldly experiences (cf. the prevalent understanding of the attribution of unchangeability, impassibility, eternity and simplicity to God), pantheism tends to have difficulty in distinguishing between the divine and the non-divine. In contrast to these positions, but incorporating the valid insights in each of them, panentheism recognizes that God and the constituents of the world have separate identities and, in particular, that God and human beings are self-conscious of their personal individuality, while maintaining that all that exists is contained within the divine (cf. Pailin 1989: chapters 5 and 10). This is what the term 'panentheism' (i.e., 'all-in-God') means.

God is therefore not to be conceived as a timeless and non-spatial reality that is essentially separate from the space-time cosmos in which we find ourselves. Models of God and the world which imply that in some way we are 'here' and God 'there', however rapid and complete the communication between these two 'locations', are misleading. There is no 'here' and no 'now' where God is not immediately present. All events in their moment of being actual, whatever their spatial and temporal separations, are events that are intrinsic parts of God's experience of the divine reality. In this respect, the world may be said to be God's 'body', especially when it is also recognized that as self-conscious beings we are able to distance ourselves from our bodies and to think about how we should respond to their states. For example, while I am in fundamental ways constituted by my body, I can also decide that I ought to reduce its bulk by slimming, or to have a diseased part of it removed, or to try to keep my emotions under better control. Just as the 'I' that makes these judgements makes judgements about what are constituent parts of itself (and the ability to do this is what is significant about self-consciousness), so God is not to be regarded as a helpless cipher for all that happens to be, but as one who is also self-consciously independent of the experiences contributed to the divine reality by the world as God's body.

Events in time and space, then, are interconnected in God. Since, furthermore, God is supremely characterized as one who loves, God may be said to be the loving environment in which each of us exists. It is this realization that formed the faith, as I interpret it, which upheld Richard Hanson as he conquered the cancer which killed him. He conquered it because he did not let it crush him. He could relax, whatever the threats, because he was confident that he was embraced by God. It is this realization which converts belief about God from being an intellectually interesting idea into a faith by which people can live as those who are open to the fundamental graciousness of reality.

As has already been noted in this study, God does not determine everything that occurs. That God is creator is not to be interpreted as implying that God is the irresistible controller of the processes of reality. Many events are the outworking of regular patterns of natural behaviour ('the laws of nature'), others (particularly at the quantum level) happen by chance, and some are the result of choices made by conscious agents. Nevertheless, because God's love is all-embracing and unlimited, everything occurs within the ambit of divine love, and every quality of everything that occurs is experienced by God. Consequently suggestions that the divine consciousness is a state of undisturbed and undisturbable bliss are mistaken.

While in some respects God's love is a warm cherishing that knows and cares for each person as that individual, it is also actualized in compassion that is scarred by deep pain. Whenever and whatever anyone suffers, God shares that suffering. The divine suffering, furthermore, is not diminished by the fact that in certain respects God must perceive what is felt by the sufferer from a wider perspective than is possible to the sufferer. Just as a father may perceive that what is frightening his child need not be feared, so God may know that what is terrifying us on some occasion does not justify that response. Nevertheless, the fear is real enough, and however limited may be a human father's empathy with his child, God's empathy is absolute. God knows what we feel just as we feel it.

When, therefore, a person suffers, whether from the ill-will of others or from the outworking of natural processes, God too suffers. The divine love is costly. When a parent worries about a sick child, when a patient lies in pain through the night, when an old man fears becoming a burden to his relatives, when a homeless young person feels that nobody cares, when a wife senses that she is despised by her husband, when a baby cries for its mother, when a friend is betrayed, when a prisoner is tortured, there too God is hurt. In this respect there are two subjects to each human experience: the human and the divine. To hold, as many Christian theologians have held, that God's being is an impassible state of utter bliss is a fundamental mis-understanding of the Christian doctrine that God is love. The image of the crucified Jesus and the use of the notion of the suffering servant of Isaiah to interpret that figure points to what God's love demands of God.

This understanding of God underlies the theology of human being that has been put forward in the previous chapters. It is now time to bring the study to a conclusion and to return, in particular, to Alex. It is his 'gentle touch' that has provoked my reflections – but he is in no way to blame for the conclusions which I have arrived at! What he has done is to make me think hard about what the Christian gospel means for all human beings. What is the 'liberation' of the children of God that is true for him as for all other finite persons?

The first step towards the liberation of any person is to give them dignity. This is what God gives to each of us, whatever our condition. God cares for each person as that distinct individual and, embracing her or him within the divine reality, imparts worth and holiness to him or her. What Isaiah affirmed to be 'the word of the Lord' to the nation as the family of God applies to every person: 'I have called you by name and you are my own' (Isaiah 43.1). It is a truth that is recognized in every sacrament of baptism as the individual is recognized by his or her own name, and in each Eucharist as the elements are given to each individual. In the central acts of Christian worship it is thus symbolically announced that God calls this person – and every person – by name and thereby gives to each person the ultimate dignity of being recognized as that individual.

The second step towards the liberation of each person is the recognition that no one is ever alone. Whatever a person experiences, however a person feels, it is also experienced and felt by God. In the story of Jesus as the Christ, God is presented as the one who identifies Godself with every person, with the victims as well as the victors, with the outcasts as well as the established, with the distressed and distraught as well as with the confident and believing. No one lives or dies, flourishes or withers, experiences joy or suffering alone. God embraces each person as that particular individual with those particular experiences, and in the divine reality the memory of each of those experiences is for ever cherished. And, it must never be overlooked, what is true of each person is true of each handicapped person; and what is true of each handicapped person is true of Alex.

This understanding of Christian faith is expressed in a hymn by Gerard Markland based on Isaiah 43.1–4:

> Do not be afraid
> for I have redeemed you.
> I have called you by your name;
> you are mine.

In the verses God promises to be with his child in 'the waters' and 'the fire' and 'the fear of loneliness', for God loves that child 'with a perfect love'. It is a hymn that was sung at Alex's baptism and at his funeral.

Alex may never have understood conceptually what those words affirm. That does not matter. He could experience the reality of what they express through the love with which others surrounded him. Furthermore, nothing at all ever happened to Alex alone. His every experience was shared by God. Whatever he might have felt, he was never alone in his pain and bewilderment and anxiety. And all his experiences, the sad and the happy, form a permanent part of the divine reality. While human memories of him dim with the passage of time, in God's awareness they have all the vividness they ever had. The fun of blowing baby-food-laced bubbles over my spectacles is still fun there! As for the dignity that was inalienably his, this was recognized to be his when he was given a name. While he provoked this study of the theology of human being and, by doing this, has been treated in some ways as a representative figure, it must never be forgotten that he was and is Alex. When I proposed writing this book and talked to his parents about it, his mother expressed proper reservations about 'using' Alex in a way that overlooked his unique personality. I hope that this has not been done. No person, whether handicapped or not, is to be thought of simply as a member of a class. God gives each the dignity symbolized by having a name: faith demands that we do the same. A theology of human being has fundamentally failed if it fails to recognize this.

The message of the hymn, 'Do not be afraid for I have redeemed you. I have called you by your name; you are mine,' is not restricted to those who are handicapped. It applies to all persons. Often those who do not consider themselves to be handicapped show themselves to be afraid of those who are. This may be because they perceive in handicapped people, albeit generally unconsciously, an undesirable and frightening symbol of their own finitude. The basic reason why handicapped people are considered to present a problem for faith in God may thus be in large part the consequence of the fact that they bring home to us that we are not God. We are finite beings. We have limited capacities and the duration of our existence on the earth is restricted. This finitude is basic to our reality as human beings. Although we still find it psychologically hard to come to terms with what Copernicus discerned, we are not the centre of the universe. That is God's place – except that that divine centre is everywhere!

Faced by our finitude, we need to be reassured by the promise, 'Do not be afraid . . . you are mine.' The fact that we do not share the infinite capacities and unending reality of God does not mean that we have no worth and that our lives have no significance. If I am correct in the understanding of Christian faith in God which I have put forward in this study, the worth of each person ultimately lies in the all-embracing love of God for that person. It is in recognizing both that we are finite and that we are taken into the infinite reality of God that we come to the true self-understanding of faith – and to true peace.

Who is the God in whom we find peace? A picture which I remember of Alex is of a glorious attempt to smile and to blow bubbles at the same time – it was glorious because it was a person-to-person contact of shared love. It is such experience of love that points us through and beyond our human encounters to God, and to God's encounter with each of us.

Who is God? The sense of the reality of God is the awareness of mystery and joy. The mystery reminds us that we are finite and that our attempts to perceive the ultimate are limited attempts to grasp what lies at the boundaries and beyond our understanding. The stories that theologians tell are stories. But they are also the best way that human beings can grasp the reality of that on which all being rests and by which we are given significance. The joy is more than a sense of happiness. It is a sense of the reality of pure goodness which profoundly loves all that is. It is in this reality that we find our peace. It is in this reality that Alex is for ever. It is in this reality that each of us lives. Be not afraid.

Works cited

Anselm, 1962: *Basic Writings*, translated by S. N. Deane, La Salle, Illinois: Open Court.

Bonhoeffer, Dietrich, 1959: *The Cost of Discipleship*, London: SCM Press.

— — 1963: *Sanctorum Communio: A Dogmatic Inquiry into the Sociology of the Church*, London: Collins.

— — 1971: *Letters and Papers from Prison*, edited by E. Bethge, London: SCM Press.

Brooke, Rupert, 1942: *The Complete Poems*, London: Sidgwick and Jackson.

Coleridge, Samuel Taylor, 1912: *The Poems of Samuel Taylor Coleridge*, edited by E. H. Coleridge, London: Oxford University Press.

Daly, Mary, 1973: *Beyond God the Father: Toward a Philosophy of Women's Liberation*, Boston: Beacon Press.

Dostoyevsky, Fyodor, 1964: *The Brothers Karamazov*, London: Folio Society.

Green, Garrett, 1989: *Imagining God: Theology and the Religious Imagination*, San Francisco: Harper and Row.

Hartshorne, Charles, 1962: *The Logic of Perfection and Other Essays in Neoclassical Metaphysics*, La Salle, Illinois: Open Court.

Herbert, Edward, Lord Herbert of Cherbury, 1705: *The Antient Religion of the Gentiles and Causes of their Errors Consider'd*, London: John Knott.

— — 1886: *The Autobiography of Edward, Lord Herbert of Cherbury*, edited by S. L. Lee, London: John C. Nimmo.

— — 1937: *De Veritate*, edited by M. H. Carré, Bristol: J. W. Arrowsmith for the University of Bristol.

Hick, John, 1968: *Evil and the God of Love*, London: Collins.

Hobbes, Thomas, n.d.: *Leviathan or the Matter, Forme and Power of a Commonwealth, Ecclesiasticall and Civil*, edited by M. Oakshott, Oxford: Basil Blackwell.

Hume, David, 1935: *Dialogues concerning Natural Religion*, edited by N. K. Smith, Oxford: Clarendon Press.

Julian of Norwich, 1980: *The Revelations of Divine Love*, translated by James Walsh, Wheathampstead, Hertfordshire: Anthony Clarke Books.

Kant, Immanuel, 1959: 'What Is Enlightenment?' in *Foundations of the Metaphysics of Morals*, edited by L. W. Beck, Indianapolis: The Library of Liberal Arts, Bobbs-Merrill.

Kierkegaard, Søren, 1955: *Fear and Trembling and Sickness Unto Death*, New York: Doubleday Anchor.

Locke, John, 1690: *An Essay concerning Human Understanding*, London: by Eliz. Holt for Thomas Bassett.

Marx, Karl, 1957: 'Theses on Feuerbach' printed in K. Marx and F. Engels, *On Religion*, Moscow: Foreign Languages Publishing House.

Mill, John Stuart, 1874: *Three Essays on Religion: Nature, The Utility of Religion and Theism*, London: Longmans, Green, Reader, and Dyer.

Monod, Jacques, 1972: *Chance and Necessity: An Essay on the Natural Philosophy of Modern Biology*, London: Collins.

Newman, John Henry, 1890: *An Essay on the Development of Christian Doctrine*, London: Longmans, Green and Co.

—— 1956: *Apologia Pro Vita Sua*, edited by A. Dwight Culler, Boston: Houghton Mifflin.

—— 1985: *An Essay in Aid of a Grammar of Assent*, edited by I. T. Ker, Oxford: Clarendon Press.

Niebuhr, H. Richard, 1961: *Radical Monotheism and Western Culture*, London: Faber and Faber.

Nietzsche, Friedrich, 1974: *The Gay Science*, New York: Vintage Books.

Ogden, Schubert M., 1967: *The Reality of God and Other Essays*, London: SCM Press.

—— 1989: *Faith and Freedom: Toward a Theology of Liberation*, revised edition, Nashville, Tennessee: Abingdon Press.

Pailin, David A., 1969: *The Way to Faith: An Examination of Newman's Grammar of Assent as a Response to the Search for Certainty in Faith*, London: Epworth Press.

—— 1986: *Groundwork of Philosophy of Religion*, London: Epworth Press.

—— 1988: 'The Poet of Salvation' printed in *Freedom and Grace* edited by Ivor H. Jones and Kenneth B. Wilson, London: Epworth Press.

—— 1989: *God and the Processes of Reality: Foundations of a Credible Theism*, London and New York: Routledge.

—— 1990: *The Anthropological Character of Theology: Conditioning Theological Understanding*, Cambridge: Cambridge University Press.

—— 1991: 'The Doctrine of Atonement: Does it rest on a misunderstanding?' in *Epworth Review*, September 1991.

Paley, William, 1837: *Natural Theology* in *The Works of William*

Paley, D.D., vol. 4, London: George Cowie and Co.

Pannenberg, Wolfhart, 1971: *Basic Questions in Theology*, vol. 3, London: SCM Press.

Peacocke, Arthur R., 1979: *Creation and the World of Science*, Oxford: Clarendon Press.

— — 1986: *God and the New Biology*, London and Melbourne: J. M. Dent.

— — 1990: *Theology for a Scientific Age*, Oxford: Basil Blackwell.

Polanyi, Michael, 1958: *Personal Knowledge: Towards a Post-Critical Philosophy*, London: Routledge and Kegan Paul.

— — 1959: *The Study of Man*, London: Routledge and Kegan Paul.

— — 1967: *The Tacit Dimension*, London: Routledge and Kegan Paul.

Ramsey, Ian T., 1964: *Models and Mystery*, London: Oxford University Press.

— — 1965: *Christian Discourse: Some Logical Explorations*, London: Oxford University Press.

Ray, John, 1722: *The Wisdom of God Manifested in the Works of the Creation*, eighth edition, London: William and John Innys.

Russell, Letty M., 1974: *Human Liberation in a Feminist Perspective — A Theology*, Philadelphia: The Westminster Press.

Sartre, Jean-Paul, 1948: *Existentialism and Humanism*, London: Methuen.

Schleiermacher, Friedrich D. E., 1928: *The Christian Faith*, edited by H. R. Mackintosh and J. S. Stewart, Edinburgh: T. & T. Clark.

Suchocki, Marjorie Hewitt, 1987: 'In Search of Justice: Religious Pluralism from a Feminist Perspective', in *The Myth of Christian Uniqueness*, edited by John Hick and Paul F. Knitter, London: SCM Press.

Tillich, Paul, 1951: *Systematic Theology*, vol. 1, London: Nisbet.

Toulmin, Stephen, 1958: *The Uses of Argument*, Cambridge: Cambridge University Press.

Underhill, Evelyn (Mrs Stuart Moore) 1917: 'Immanence', printed in *The Oxford Book of English Mystical Verse*, chosen by D. H. S. Nicholson and A. H. E. Lee, Oxford: Clarendon Press.

Voltaire, 1947: *Candide*, translated by J. Butt, Harmondsworth: Penguin Books.

— — 1962: *Philosophical Dictionary*, edited by Peter Gay, New York: Harcourt, Brace and World.

Wesley, John, 1819: *The Works*, vol. 2, London: by T. Cordeux for T. Blanshard.

— — 1820: *The Works*, vol. 7, London: by T. Cordeux for T. Blanshard.

Whitehead, Alfred North, 1978: *Process and Reality: An Essay in Cosmology*, corrected edition edited by D. R. Griffin and D. W.

Sherburne, New York: The Free Press.

Williams, H. A., 1965: *The True Wilderness*, London: Constable.

Wittgenstein, Ludwig, 1963: *Tractatus Logico-Philosophicus*, London: Routledge and Kegan Paul.

Index